*A Historical
Sketch of Liberty
and Equality*

Frederic William Maitland

A Historical Sketch of Liberty and Equality

AS IDEALS OF
ENGLISH POLITICAL PHILOSOPHY
FROM THE TIME OF HOBBES
TO THE TIME OF COLERIDGE

Frederic William Maitland

LIBERTY FUND

INDIANAPOLIS

© 2000 by Liberty Fund, Inc. All rights reserved.

"The Historical Spirit Incarnate: Frederic William Maitland," by Robert Livingston Schuyler, was originally published in *American Historical Review* 57, no. 2 (January 1952): 303–22, and is reprinted here by permission of the American Historical Association.

Frontispiece by courtesy of the National Portrait Gallery, London

Printed in the United States of America

05 04 03 02 01 C 5 4 3 2 1
05 04 03 02 01 P 5 4 3 2 1

Library of Congress Cataloging-in-Publication Data

Maitland, Frederic William, 1850–1906.
[Historical sketch of liberty and equality as ideals of English political philosophy from the time of Hobbes to the time of Coleridge]
A historical sketch of liberty and equality/F. W. Maitland.
p.   cm.
Includes bibliographical references and index.
ISBN 0–86597–292–3 (hc: alk. paper)—ISBN 0–86597–293–1 (pbk: alk. paper)
1. Political science—Great Britain—History.   2. Liberty—History.
3. Equality—History.
I. Title.
JA84.G7 .M35   2001
323'.01—dc21   00–027491

Liberty Fund, Inc.
8335 Allison Pointe Trail, Suite 300
Indianapolis, Indiana 46250–1684

CONTENTS

NOTE ON THE TEXT

"A Historical Sketch of Liberty and Equality" was composed by Frederic William Maitland as a dissertation for a fellowship at Trinity College, Cambridge, in 1875, when the author was twenty-five years old. The essay was included in *The Collected Works of Frederic W. Maitland* published by Cambridge University Press in 1911. The Liberty Fund edition of Maitland's essay appears as it was originally published, with no elaboration on the footnotes, aside from translation as noted below. In keeping with the nature of the essay—a dissertation—the footnotes assume considerable learning upon the part of the reader and refer to contemporaneous editions of the cited works. To ensure that the essay itself is accessible to the general reader in an era when knowledge of classical languages is no longer the rule, pertinent passages in French, German, or Greek have been translated into English, enclosed in brackets. The translations were executed by Dennis O'Keeffe, Dan Kirklin, and Chris Oleson, respectively. Also included in this volume is "The Body Politic," a lecture that is typical of the author's application of his methods to his own historical period.

A Historical Sketch of Liberty and Equality

Frederic William Maitland
(1850–1906)

FOREIGN HONORARY MEMBER IN

CLASS III, SECTION I, 1897

Frederic William Maitland was born in London 28 May 1850 and died at Las Palmas, Canaries, 19 December 1906. The grandson of Samuel R. Maitland, the historian of the "Dark Ages," he was educated at Eton and Trinity College, Cambridge, where he came under the influence of Henry Sidgwick and won high distinction in philosophy. He entered Lincoln's Inn in 1872 and was called to the bar in 1876. His interests, however, soon began to turn from the practice of law to its history, and in 1884 he was appointed Reader of English Law in the University of Cambridge, and in 1888 Downing Professor of the Laws of England, a chair which he held until his death. It is, however, characteristic of the English university system that

This essay was originally published in *Proceedings of the American Academy of Arts and Sciences* 51, no. 14 (1916): 904–5.

the duties of his professorship consisted of general lectures to undergraduates on the elements of law rather than of the training of scholars in his special field, so that he formed no school of disciples who could develop or continue his work. His professorship, however, gave him considerable leisure for writing, and in spite of the ill health which soon drove him southward in the winter and finally cut him off in the fulness of his activity, he accomplished an astonishing amount of productive labor.

It is a curious fact that Maitland owed to a Russian historian, Paul Vinogradoff, his introduction to the original records of English legal history. The acquaintance ripened speedily into his first important publication, a roll of "Pleas of the Crown for the County of Gloucester" in 1884, followed in 1887 by "Bracton's Note-book." Then came "Select Pleas of the Crown" (1888); "Select Pleas in Manorial Courts" (1889); "Three Rolls of the King's Court, 1194–5" (1891); "Records of the Parliament of 1305" (1893); "The Mirror of Justices" (1895); "Select Passages from Bracton and Azo" (1895); and the "Year Books of Edward II," as far as 1310 (1903–06). Merely as an editor of records and as the prime mover in inaugurating the publications of the Selden Society, he would hold a high place among those who have advanced the cause of English history. He shrank from no editorial labor, such as the difficult problems of the Law-French of the Year Books, but his introductions also show the wide learning, the luminous view, and the brilliant style which characterize all his writings. Besides these editions and a number of scattered essays, most of which have been brought together into the three volumes of his "Collected Papers," his most important works are "Domesday Book and Beyond" (1897); "Township and Borough" (1898); "Roman Canon Law in the Church of England" (1898); a translation of Gierke's "Political Theories of the Middle Ages" (1900); a brilliant lecture on "English Law and the Renaissance" (1901); a posthumous set of lectures on "The Constitutional History of England" (1908); and the classic "History of English Law before the Time of Edward I" (1895), published conjointly with Sir Frederick Pollock but chiefly the work of Maitland. His last weeks in Cambridge were given to the "Life and Letters of Leslie Stephen." A full bibliography of his writings is appended to A. L. Smith's *Frederic William Maitland* (Oxford, 1908), where many characteristic passages are quoted. A biography, with a number of letters illustrating his style and the charm of his personality, has been published by Herbert Fisher (Cambridge, 1910).

As an historian of English law Maitland has never been equalled. He was a finished jurist without the lawyer's reverence for form and authority; he combined the philosopher's power of analysis with the faculty of seeing everything in the concrete; and he had the delicate sense of evidence, the flashing insight, the vivid imagination, and the human sympathy of the great historian. To him the history of law was the history, not of forms, but of ideas; through it "the thoughts of men in the past must once more become thinkable to us." Yet law is not something abstract: its records "come from life," as he said of the Year Books, and must return to life. "English law is English history," he wrote; yet, first of English scholars, he saw it clearly against its Continental background. Unlike many jurists, however, he did not seek to reduce the manifold complexities of life to a few general principles and to clarify what had never been clear; he avoided too definite conclusions and rather let his mind play about a subject in all its variety and illuminate it from different angles. To a masterly gift of exposition and a talent for apt illustration he joined a marvellous style, pointed, witty, epigrammatic, lighting up the dullest and most technical subject, and adorning everything it touched. Confining himself to the history of institutions and ideas, he did not enter the field of the narrative historian, so that the absence of a common standard renders comparisons difficult; but the quality of his mind justifies Lord Acton's judgment that he was "the ablest historian in England."

CHARLES H. HASKINS

The Historical Spirit Incarnate: Frederic William Maitland

The hundredth anniversary of the birth of Frederic William Maitland fell in 1950. There is, however, a better reason than belated centennialism for pausing to consider what he stood for as a historian because what he stood for, unless I am much mistaken, needs to be emphasized today. Maitland has a message not only for professional students, teachers, and writers of history but for everybody who aspires to balance and sanity in his attitude toward the past. If a confession of historiographical faith on my part can be found in what I am going to say about him, this is something that will not greatly concern anyone but me. Yet it should perhaps be stated explicitly at the outset, rather than left to be inferred by you later, that Maitland has meant more to me than any other historian—not primarily for the subjects he dealt with, but for his methods, his insights, and his superb historical sense. He was a lawyer, and his specialty

Presidential address read at the annual dinner of the American Historical Association in New York on December 29, 1951.

was the history of English law, though he did original and important work in other branches of history. But it would be wrong to think of him as just a lawyer who happened to become interested in the history of his subject. He was, rather, what his intimate friend and collaborator Sir Frederick Pollock called him, "a man with a genius for history, who turned its light upon law because law, being his profession, came naturally into the field." As a professor of legal history at Cambridge, he used medieval law as a tool to "open . . . the mind of medieval man and to reveal the nature and growth of his institutions," as one of his students, George Macaulay Trevelyan, has told us. I doubt whether any medievalist has ever made a more earnest and sustained effort to get inside the medieval mind.

The only one of Maitland's forebears who needs to be spoken of here is his grandfather, the Reverend Samuel Roffey Maitland, who was librarian to the archbishop of Canterbury at Lambeth Palace and wrote a number of books, mainly on medieval religious history. As a boy Frederic William visited from time to time at Maitland House, his grandfather's home in Gloucestershire, and later he came to have a great admiration for his historical writings. There were, in fact, striking resemblances between grandfather and grandson considered as historians.

The elder Maitland was never content to stop short of the most reliable available original sources for his historical knowledge, and he was distinctly critical, exceptionally so for his day, in handling historical evidence. He was, therefore, skeptical in his attitude toward historical traditions. As a medievalist he had a strong feeling for the general cultural context in which the institutions of the Middle Ages were embedded, and he was keenly sensitive to the differences between it and the cultural milieu of his own day—which is to say that he was historically-minded, and, being so, he was repelled by anachronism. He liked the medieval in the Middle Ages but not in modern times. Thus he had good things to say about medieval monasticism, but its merits in its own day were not, in his opinion, a valid reason for reviving the monastic system in nineteenth-century England, as had recently been proposed. Indeed, he did not believe that the *medieval* monastic system could be revived.

We have been hearing so much of late about subjectivity and objectivity in historianship, about the historian's "frame of reference" and "controlling assumptions," about history as faith *versus* history as science, that we may be in some danger of supposing that thought on such subjects is an exclusively twentieth-century form of cerebration. Samuel Roffey Maitland lived long before the term "historical relativism" had been coined, but in his historical outlook he was a thorough relativist. He understood quite clearly that the institutions of the past could be comprehended only when viewed in their context, and he knew equally well that a man of the nineteenth century, even if he was a historian, could not become absolutely and consistently medieval. Here is a remark of his that could serve as a text for a discourse on historical relativism at a meeting of historians today: "Do what he may, no man can strip himself of the circumstances, and concomitants, which it has pleased God to place around him." Frederic William Maitland's indebtedness to his grandfather's critical methods and historical point of view was undoubtedly very considerable. A private letter of his, written early in his career as a historian, tells us as much.

As a student at Cambridge, where his earliest interests—in music, mathematics, and athletics—had little enough obvious relation to what was to be his lifework, Maitland before long came under the influence of the eminent philosopher, and professor of philosophy, Henry Sidgwick, with results of importance for his intellectual development. He read widely in various branches of philosophy, and to such good purpose that he came out at the head of the first class in the Moral and Mental Science Tripos of 1872. He acquired a reputation as a humorous and brilliant talker and an extremely effective public speaker, and already as an undergraduate he gave more than a hint of that flair for pointing an argument with an epigram that was to characterize his lecturing and writing in after years.

Maitland entered Lincoln's Inn in 1872 and was called to the bar in 1876. In the law chambers of Benjamin Bickley Rogers, who is still remembered in classical circles for the translations of the comedies of Aristophanes with which he beguiled his leisure hours, the young barrister specialized in conveyancing, and his familiarity with that highly technical branch of English law served him well in his later study of early English land deeds and charters. The testimony of Mr. Rogers is eloquent as to Maitland's extraordinary legal talents: "he had not been with me a week before I found that I had in my chambers such a lawyer as I had never met before. . . . his opinions, had he suddenly been made a judge, would have been an honour to the Bench."

Many lawyers have written history, and often, in sorrow be it added, quite untruthful history. The time-honored method of studying law, in English inns of court and American law schools, has not made for historical-mindedness. The lawyer is concerned with precedents, to be sure, but usually not with the context of his precedents. If, to quote some penetrating words that I have seen ascribed to my old friend Reed Powell, who has devoted his years of discretion to the study of how judges think, "If you think that you can think about a thing, inextricably attached to something else, without thinking of the thing it is attached to, then you have a legal mind." The historical mind, on the other hand, sees past events in their contemporary contexts. In his inaugural lecture as Downing Professor of the Laws of England at Cambridge, delivered in October, 1888, and entitled "Why the History of English Law Is Not Written," Maitland, with characteristic insight, thus contrasted the legal mind and the historical mind:

> . . . what is really required of the practising lawyer is not, save in the rarest cases, a knowledge of medieval law as it was in the Middle Ages, but rather a knowledge of medieval law as interpreted by modern courts to suit modern facts. A lawyer finds on his table a case about rights of common which sends him to the Statute of Merton. But is it really the law of 1236 that he wants to know? No, it is the ultimate result of the interpretations set on the statute by the judges of twenty generations. The more modern the decision, the more valuable for his purpose. That process by which old principles and old phrases are charged with a new content, is from the lawyer's point of view an evolution of the true intent and meaning of the old law; from the historian's point of view it is almost of necessity a process of perversion and misunderstanding.

Let me underscore one phrase in that quotation; we shall be coming back to it: *a knowledge of medieval law as it was in the Middle Ages.*

As a young man, and in fact throughout his life, Maitland took a lively interest in current affairs, though he did not find time to write much on them. For it was a settled conviction of his—in the opinion of some, this may be thought to date him—that the highest function of a historian is to be a historian. Law reform, however, was one of his early and abiding interests. His approach to the subject was historical, as we should expect, and his attitude toward it decidedly radical. As a young conveyancer, he declared in an article published in 1879 that what was needed was "nothing less than a total abolition of all that is distinctive in real property law," and it was his mature judgment, expressed toward the end of his life, that the historical spirit, far from being the handmaid of conservatism, was the natural ally of rational reform. He was spiritually akin to the great English law reformers of the early nineteenth century, and he could use equally vigorous language. He belonged in what Sir William Holdsworth called the "long series of judges, conveyancers, and legislators" whose efforts led to the drastic reforms in English property law in the 1920's. He was ever a sworn foe of what he called "out-worn theories and obsolescent ideas," though it should quickly be added that his historical sense prevented him from making the crude mistake of condemning theories or ideas in the past because they later became incumbrances and impediments. In connection with the law of real property he spoke of the need of clearing up what he called "that great medieval muddle which passes under the name of feudalism," but he never expressed contempt for feudalism in the feudal ages. He did not endorse what he described as "the cheerful optimism which refuses to see that the process of civilization is often a cruel process," but on the other hand he never beheld myopic visions of golden ages in the good old days.

Two of Maitland's contemporaries, both of them close personal friends of his, did much to determine his lifework. One of these was Frederick Pollock, whose name is always linked with his. Pollock was a few years older than Maitland and preceded him by a few years in the educational procession—at Eton, Trinity College, Cambridge, and Lincoln's Inn. Maitland has recorded that it was through Pollock that his interest in legal history was first aroused. The two friends collaborated in writing the treatise that has been a classic in English legal history for more than a half-century, *The History of English Law before the Time of Edward I,* always cited as "Pollock and Maitland." The order in which the authors' names appeared on the title page was in accordance with professional legal usage, the order, namely, of seniority at the bar, but a note by Pollock, added to the preface, recorded that Maitland's share in the work, both as to research and as to composition, was by far the greater. One of my predecessors in this chair, who was also my old chief at Yale, George Burton Adams, pronounced "Pollock and Maitland" to be unequaled as a work of continuous institutional history—and Professor Adams was not addicted to uncritical eulogy.

The other friend whose influence on Maitland was very great was the Russian medievalist Paul Vinogradoff. Visiting England in search of materials for medieval history, Vinogradoff became greatly impressed by the immense stores of unexploited archive sources for English legal history in the Public Record Office in London. Meeting Maitland by chance in January, 1884, he communicated his enthusiasm to him, with results that were to be decisive in Maitland's career and momentous for the history of English law. "I often think," Maitland wrote to Vinogradoff some years later, "what an extraordinary piece of luck for me it was that you and I met upon a 'Sunday tramp.' That day determined the rest of my life." The first fruit of Maitland's enthusiastic explorations at the Public Record Office was an edition of an early thirteenth-century plea roll, which he published before the end of 1884, with a masterly introduction and an appropriate dedication to Vinogradoff. He had now entered on his lifework as a legal historian.

In that same year, 1884, Maitland began to teach at Cambridge. Four years later he was elected Downing Professor of the Laws of England, and he held this chair for the rest of his life. As a lecturer he was pre-eminently original—illuminating, suggestive, and stimulating in what he had to say, which was carefully prepared, and impressive, humorous, and even at times dramatic in his manner of saying it. Students spoke of his power to create historical atmosphere and make dry bones live. In addition to formal lectures he used to give informal instruction in paleography and diplomatics to small groups of advanced students. My colleague Professor Shotwell, who knew Maitland in his later years and was familiar with the character and quality of his teaching, has spoken of this work of his as a kind of informal Ecole des Chartes.

In 1887 the Selden Society was founded for the purpose of advancing the knowledge of English law by publishing first-hand materials for the study of its history. Maitland was the prime mover in its establishment, became its literary director, and remained its inspiring genius until his death. Twenty-one volumes were issued by the society during his lifetime, of which eight were his own contributions, and all the others, some of them undertaken at his suggestion, underwent his editorial supervision. As a historical editor he was the opposite of perfunctory, and his introductions to his own volumes have been a boon to students because of his lucid presentation of his findings, his clear-visioned insights, his original and ingenious hypotheses, and his critical historical methods.

After all the argument and controversy that have been raging in historical circles regarding the uses and objectives of historical study, the nature of historical knowledge, and that perennially alluring apple of discord, historical relativism, most of us still speak respectfully, if not enthusiastically, about historical truth—that is, when we speak of it at all. Some of us are old enough to have listened to the impressive and beautiful address on "Truth in History" read before this Association nearly forty years ago by its President, my old and honored teacher, William Archibald Dunning, and all of us could read it with profit.

Only a selfless dedication to historical truth could have sustained labors so laborious and pains so painful as those to which Maitland subjected himself. A single instance must suffice for illustration. He turned from a continuation of *The History of English Law*, which he had much at heart, to the preparation of a critical edition of early Year Books because he regarded this latter as an indispensable preliminary to the former. To an understanding of the Year Books, however, there was also an indispensable preliminary—a thorough knowledge of the language in which they were written, the Anglo-French language spoken in English law courts in the thirteenth and fourteenth centuries. And hence our historian turned grammarian, orthographer, and phoneticist. For the competence with which he performed this exacting and intensely laborious task we have the testimony of a distinguished contemporary French philologist, who recommended Maitland's excursion into medieval law French, published in the introduction to the first volume of the Year Books which he edited for the Selden Society, to all students of Old French in any of its numerous varieties. Maitland's achievement seems all the more remarkable in that he took no interest in philology for its own sake and that his work on the Year Books was done in the closing years of his life, under the

severe handicap of illness and enforced absences from England.
He retained to the very end his capacity for the drudgery involved in scholarship. The pursuit of historical truth, as he understood that term, was Maitland's ruling passion, and it ex-
plains, I think, most of his traits as a historian.

Anyone who has read more than a very little of Maitland is sure
to be impressed by his concreteness and mastery of detail. He
had a healthy distrust of the glittering generality that disdains
illustration for he knew that concrete events are the stuff of history. One of the chief virtues of Stubbs's *Constitutional History
of England*, in his judgment, was a concreteness exceptional in
books on that subject. "People can't understand old law," he
once remarked, "unless you give a few concrete illustrations; at
least I can't." And so his writing is alive with facts and the doings of men, even though the men are sometimes necessarily
left anonymous. He never forgot that human institutions and
ideas have no existence, no life of their own, apart from human beings.

This concreteness of Maitland's, his factualism, goes far, if it
does not go all the way, to explain his historical interpretations
and conceptions of causation. You will search his writings in
vain for any reference to historical laws, universal determinism
of any variety (providential, economic, racial, geographical,
or other), controlling social forces, or *Zeitgeister*. He himself,
when young, had eagerly pursued philosophy as an academic
subject, to be sure, and he must have heard great argument
about causation, but the bent of his genius was historical. Perhaps he was too essentially and wholeheartedly the historian to
take kindly to historical philosophy. You can find some "necessary conditions" in Maitland, but he did not misspend time and
energy in the futile attempt to establish "fundamental causes."

He knew that causation in history is always multiple and complex, and that among antecedents there are always events that look like historical accidents, events, that is to say, which it seems impossible to account for as even probable results of *their known antecedents.* He was never guilty of the folly of brushing aside as useless or vain, conjectures on the part of historians in response to hypothetical questions contrary to historical fact. Without such conjectures, indeed, it would seem to be impossible to form any estimate of the significance of events and personalities in history, and he himself engaged explicitly in them. For example, in a passage in *The History of English Law* dealing with the results of the Norman Conquest in English legal history he asks whether a charter of liberties would ever have been granted in England if William the Conqueror had left only one son instead of three. And again, in his *English Law and the Renaissance,* where he is speaking of what he considered to be England's narrow "escape" from a reception of Roman law in the middle years of the sixteenth century, he says:

> If Reginald Pole's dream had come true, if there had been a Reception—well, I have not the power to guess and you have not the time to hear what would have happened; but I think that we should have had to rewrite a great deal of history. For example, in the seventeenth century there might have been a struggle between king and parliament, but it would hardly have been that struggle for the medieval, the Lancastrian, constitution in which Coke and Selden and Prynne and other ardent searchers of mouldering records won their right to be known to schoolboys.

With all his concreteness, however, Maitland was not bogged down in detail so as to be incapable of generalization. On the contrary, he exhibited the rare combination of mastery of detail and high generalizing power, though he knew that most historical generalizations need qualification. Generalization is constantly in evidence in his writings. It is shown in surveys such as his article on the history of English law in the eleventh edition of the *Encyclopaedia Britannica,* it is shown in epigrams scattered through his writings. These are never mere purple patches, sewn on for ornament. They are used to drive points home, to clinch arguments.

Though primarily a legal historian, Maitland was not a narrowly legal historian. He knew, of course, that specialization, division of labor, is necessary if historical study is to advance. But no historian has perceived more clearly that the various departments into which the whole field of history, considered as knowledge about the past, has been divided for convenience and scientific utility are not severally self-sufficient or self-explanatory. No historian has felt more sensitively that this departmentalization of knowledge does not correspond to anything in history, considered as the flow of events in the past, to anything, that is to say, inherent in the historic process itself—that it tends, on the contrary, to obscure relationships that have always existed in that process as an undivided whole. He counted it for righteousness in his friend Leslie Stephen that he was "a great contemner of boundaries, whom no scheme of the sciences, no delimitation of departments, would keep in the highway if he had a mind to go across country." Maitland knew that the historian of law must often go outside his own bailiwick for explanations, and, conversely, that specialists in other historical domains should often turn to the history of law. If medievalists today make greater use of legal materials as sources for English social, economic, and constitutional history than their nineteenth-century predecessors did, some of the credit for this improvement belongs to Maitland.

Maitland's mind, like that of every other great historian, was of strongly critical cast. Constant exercise of private judgment must have strengthened the critical faculty in him, and reliance upon private judgment became very early a part of the man. There was in him, however, no tinge of arrogance or false pride of opinion. His ego never took precedence over his devotion to historical truth, and therefore he was never "exhausted in the effort to be omniscient," as has been said of Karl Marx. In religion private judgment made him a dissenter even from Dissent, and it made him, as a historian, critical in his approach to historical evidence. What he admired most in his grandfather as a historian was his critical power. Maitland's mind was of the rare type that does not take even commonplace things for granted. A useful collection of essays in historical criticism could be compiled from his writings.

Maitland's independence of judgment could not fail to bring him at times into conflict with opinions and schools of thought that enjoyed wide acceptance and the endorsement of great names. But he was not polemical by preference. He never sought controversy, I think, or rejoiced in it, like some of his predecessors—and successors. Yet he was never overawed by authority, however eminent, and he did not shrink from taking issue with historians whom he respected if he became convinced that they were in error. He was habitually considerate and generous in his attitude toward other historical scholars and always tried to think the best of their performances. His historical criticisms, according to Vinogradoff, exemplified the maxim *suaviter in modo, fortiter in re.* Only if he thought that injustice had been done did he show signs of strong feeling, and then he could be devastating, even though the injured party had been dead for half a dozen centuries.

Suggestiveness is a conspicuous characteristic of Maitland's writing. He addressed himself to a limited public, though he had no contempt for historical popularizers provided they were "honest and reasonably industrious," and he himself possessed literary gifts that could have placed him high in their ranks. In reviewing a ponderous work of Germanic historical scholarship he confessed that Gallic "high vulgarization" had its attraction for him. He was devoid of the intellectual snobbishness that values knowledge the more when it is esoteric. Still he was primarily a historians' historian, and he was always eager to aid other scholars and encourage them to labor, not in *his* vineyard (for no historian has been less monopolistic or proprietary in his attitude toward his field of specialization) but in the vineyard with him. His perception of historical problems awaiting solution and of work to be done in aid of historical scholarship made him extraordinarily fertile in suggestion, and a goodly crop of historical writing has stemmed from ideas which he threw out. To eliminate from written history, in the name of art, the evidences and inferences on which opinions have been based, to obscure the process of which the finished work is the final product, he considered to be a crime against history. He spoke with playful sarcasm of England as a land "where men are readily persuaded that hard labour is disagreeable and that the signs of hard labour are disgusting." He gave high praise to historians like Stubbs and Liebermann, who took their readers into their confidence and showed them historianship behind the scenes. Of Stubbs he said: "No other Englishman has so completely displayed to the world the whole business of the historian from the winning of the raw material to the narrating and generalising." This judgment can be applied with equal propriety to himself. Stubbs and Maitland were both historians' historians, both mighty contributors to historical knowledge, both eager to help others in advancing it, and both historical editors who carried the editorial art to its highest levels. No other series of introductions to historical sources and records—at least none in the English language—deserves to be placed abreast of Stubbs's or of Maitland's. No other English historian's footnotes have been more seminal than theirs. The dean of English medievalists of our own day, Professor Powicke, has declared that nothing can deprive the great works of these two masters of their pre-eminence.

Maitland conclusively refutes the false and mischievous notion, widely entertained though it is both in professional historical circles and by the history-reading public, that great learning and good writing are incompatible. We guild historians (with some exceptions of course) have tended to be suspicious of anything verging on style—that is, on good style. On the other hand, the esthetic sense of the public, at any rate as interpreted by commercial publishers (and few publishers known to me are wholly uncommercial), is offended by obtrusive evidences of scholarship, insisting, for example, upon the elimination of footnotes or, at least, their consignment to the rear, where those whom they may concern can examine them—with a maximum of inconvenience. Maitland had, it is true, no craving for popularity, and his appeal has not been to the general reading public, largely no doubt because of the nature of his subject matter. A chapter which he contributed to the *Cambridge Modern History,* on "The Anglican Settlement and the Scottish Reformation," shows that he could write narrative history of the first quality when he wanted to. But the historian of institutions and ideas, and this, essentially, is what he was, has never enjoyed the popular favor accorded to narrative historians. "The History of Institutions cannot be mastered,—can scarcely be approached,—without an effort"—such is the majestic sentence with which Stubbs began the preface to his *Constitutional History of England.* You simply cannot imagine *Domesday Book and Beyond* superseding the latest best-selling novel on dressing tables in young ladies' boudoirs, the ambition that Macaulay cherished for his *History.* The kind of history to which Maitland devoted himself requires for its understanding more active response, more mental effort, a higher degree of sympathetic imagination on the reader's part, than the incisive rhetoric of Macaulay or the glowing prose of John Richard Green. It is also, as Maitland came to see, more risky than narrative history. "Would Gibbon's editor," he asked, "find so few mistakes to rectify if Gibbon had seriously tried to make his readers live for a while under the laws of Franks and Lombards?"

Yet Maitland was a consummate master of the art of expressing thought in English prose. Contemporaries who were familiar with his writings were all impressed by his literary qualities; and a generation after his death the editors of a collection of his articles coupled what they called "the matchless attraction of his style" with "the brilliant scholarship and originality of thought which he brought to bear upon every topic that he handled." He had no set method, nor any single manner, of writing. He was eloquent (though never pompous) or homely (though never vulgar) or gay (though never flippant), as the nature of his subject and his mood moved him. His style, if it can be spoken of in the singular, is singularly various, but it never lacks the quality of distinction. Humor is certainly one of its salient features, humor "abounding in delightful surprises," says Pollock, "overflowing even into the titles of learned papers, breaking out in footnotes with rapid allusive touches." "Humor in footnotes" is itself a delightful surprise which I respectfully commend to the attention of my fellow members of this Association. Maitland had darts of sarcasm and irony in his armory, and he knew how to discharge them with telling effect, but his darts, however pointed, were never poisoned, and they were rarely aimed at individuals. He was well equipped with devices for fixing attention, facilitating understanding, and driving home arguments—reiteration and the use of the *leitmotif,* striking characterization, dramatic visualization, apt (and sometimes bold) literary quotation. A single example of the last, of almost audacious quotation, must suffice for illustration. In the introduction to his first major historical work, *Bracton's Note Book,* Maitland expressed the opinion that Bracton found some specific rules of Roman law handy, but that in the main he borrowed them for application in concrete cases only when there was no applicable English authority. Such a general statement was all very well, yet it might not stick. But who will forget the point after Maitland has called upon Hamlet to help him drive it in?

> Imperial Caesar dead and turned to clay
> Might stop a hole to keep the wind away.

John Fiske, in the preface to his *Discovery of America,* emphasizes the need of freeing our minds from "bondage to the modern map"—a phrase which he borrowed from Edward A. Freeman—if we wish to understand what the great mariners of the fifteenth and sixteenth centuries were seeking. "The ancient map," he says, "must take its place. . . . In dealing with the discovery of America one must steadily keep before one's mind the quaint notions of ancient geographers. . . . It was just these distorted and hazy notions that swayed the minds and guided the movements of the great discoverers." Bondage to the modern map, however, has been only one phase of bondage to the modern in general, from which the writing of history has always suffered and from which, if a counsel of perfection is permissible, it ought to be freed. The process of emancipation needs to be extended to all branches of history—the history of institutions and ideas no less than the history of geographical discovery. Maitland's clear and steady perception of this need in historiography and his fidelity to the liberating and therapeutic principle of historical-mindedness were, it seems to me, the most distinguishing factors in his greatness as a historian. His appreciation of ideological differences between past and present was plainly in evidence early in his career as a writer—in a dissertation in the field of political theory which he submitted in competition for a fellowship at Cambridge and in his earliest important contribution to legal history. His work, taken as a whole, remains a standing protest against what Professor Sayles has recently called the "perverse historical doctrine that the past could only be understood in the light of the present."

A historical conviction of Maitland's that was rooted in his historical-mindedness was often reiterated in his writings, namely, that the course of development in legal thinking has been from the vague to the definite. In a striking passage in *Domesday Book and Beyond* he put this thought in these words:

> The grown man will find it easier to think the thoughts of the school-boy than to think the thoughts of the baby. And yet the doctrine that our remote forefathers being simple folk had simple law dies hard. Too often we allow ourselves to suppose that, could we but get back to the beginning, we should find that all was intelligible and should then be able to watch the

process whereby simple ideas were smothered under subtleties and technicalities. But it is not so. Simplicity is the outcome of technical subtlety; it is the goal, not the starting point. As we go backwards the familiar outlines become blurred; the ideas become fluid, and instead of the simple we find the indefinite.

Haze, Maitland often seems to be telling us, ought to be recognized for what it was. It should be allowed to remain hazy. It should not be given the semblance of clarity by having an unhistorical and false lucidity forced upon it. The temptation to clarify medieval haze is strong in the mind of the modern historian, but it ought to be strongly resisted: "We shall have to think away distinctions which seem to us as clear as the sunshine; we must think ourselves back into a twilight. This we must do, not in a haphazard fashion, but of set purpose, knowing what we are doing."

The baffling problems of interpretation with which Maitland, as a medievalist, felt himself forced to wrestle, raised no perplexing difficulties for the medievals themselves—did not, indeed, exist for them—but that was because haze was not disturbed by haziness. There were no medievalists in the Middle Ages, there were just medievals. The medievalist is an exclusively modern phenomenon, a fact to which most of his spiritual tribulations are attributable.

Historical-mindedness, Maitland soon came to realize, was especially difficult in the field of early law and custom. It was far harder to find out what our remote ancestors thought than to find out what words they used or what implements they made. Again and again, explicitly and implicitly, he tells us that we ought not to force modern ideas on the Middle Ages. The problem in hand may be the status of the *servus* of Domesday

Book. We moderns can call him a slave, but was he thought of at the time as a thing or as a person—or as neither? "We may well doubt," Maitland's answer is, "whether this principle— "The slave is a thing, not a person'—can be fully understood by a grossly barbarous age. It implies the idea of a person, and in the world of sense we find not persons but men." Modern legal theories are, in general, too definite, modern legal distinctions too sharply drawn, to suit medieval facts. The distinction, for example, between "alodial ownership" and "feudal tenure," a sharp distinction, as modern historians had usually supposed, ought not to be pushed back too far, for in the eleventh century men were said to *hold* land *of* others *in alodio*. It was the same in the domain of political ideas and theories—"our medieval history will go astray, our history of Italy and Germany will go far astray . . . unless we both know and feel that we must not thrust our modern 'State-concept,' as a German would call it, upon the reluctant material." Sometimes Maitland's interpretations involving striking contrasts between archaic and modern ways of thinking are positively startling, as in what he has to say about Anglo-Saxon ideas of justice in relation to judicial proof by oath:

> The swearer satisfies human justice by taking the oath. If he has sworn falsely, he is exposed to the wrath of God and in some subsequent proceeding may perhaps be convicted of perjury; but in the meantime he has performed the task that the law set him; he has given the requisite proof. . . . The plaintiff, if he thought that there had been perjury, would have the satisfaction of knowing that some twelve of his enemies [the defendant's oath-helpers] were devoted to divine vengeance.

After-mindedness, that is to say, the retrojection into a past age of interests and ideas and attitudes and standards of later times, is likely, Maitland perceived, to lead us far astray in our interpretations of historical movements and tendencies, of human motives, of values in general. It may, for example, mislead us into mistaking progress for retrogression, it may persuade us that what was really contempt for a conquered people was an enlightened spirit of toleration, it may turn us topsy-turvy in our historical judgments on all kinds of questions. Even in the domain of ethics there were for Maitland no absolutes. All human conduct ought to be judged in relation to time and circumstance. Bracton, for instance, should not be accused of plagiarism because he did not conform to modern standards in acknowledging indebtedness to others. In his time nobody did. "Literary communism" was the order of the day.

Anachronism was as distasteful to Maitland, with his keen sense of time-depth, as it had been to his grandfather, and the obligation of the historian to be eternally vigilant in taking precautions against this historical disease is one of the great lessons to be learned from him. Anyone gifted with historic sense must, he felt, dislike to see a rule or an idea unfitly surviving in a changed environment.

> An anachronism should offend not only his reason, but his taste. Roman Law was all very well at Rome; medieval law in the Middle Age. But the modern man in a toga, or a coat of mail, or a chasuble, is not only uncomfortable but unlovely.

Anachronism, he perceived, often leads us to follow false scents. Many questions that have been asked about the past are unhistorical questions because they are anachronistic. It was peculiarly difficult, he realized, to avoid anachronism in the realm of ideas:

> Against many kinds of anachronism we now guard ourselves. We are careful of costume, of armour and architecture, of words

and forms of speech. But it is far easier to be careful of these things than to prevent the intrusion of untimely ideas. . . . If, for example, we introduce the *persona ficta* too soon, we shall be doing worse than if we armed Hengist and Horsa with machine guns or pictured the Venerable Bede correcting proofs for the press.

What Maitland called "antedating the emergence of modern ideas" he declared to be the "besetting sin" in the traditional attitude of the English legal profession toward medieval English legal history. It was not difficult, for example, for the modern lawyer to find corporations in England much too early—"when we turn to a far-off past we may be in great danger of too readily seeing a corporation in some group of landholders, which, if modern distinctions are to be applied at all, would be better classed as a group of joint tenants than as a corporation." We must take care, he urges us in many different connections, not to hurry history.

Antiquarianism, on the other hand, might run to excess and defeat its own purpose. Thus in the matter of orthography, Maitland's sound judgment saved him from following the example of Green, who sprinkled his pages on Anglo-Saxon England with such outlandish name-forms as Eadwine, Baeda, and Ecgberht. Maitland knew that the letter often killeth, and he felt, in all probability, that such antiquarian literalism tended to give a false impression of the bizarre and the fantastic, which impeded rather than facilitated historical comprehension. In dealing with Bracton he had to decide between the traditional spelling of his name and the spelling as it was written in Bracton's own day—"Bratton." He decided in favor of tradition: "Bracton he has been for centuries, and so let him be to the end."

Maitland knew too much history, and felt too historically about what he knew, to suppose that after-mindedness is a distinctly modern phenomenon. He knew that men in *all* ages had trodden that primrose path which has always led to anachronism, distortion, and falsification of *earlier* ages. Thus medieval English lawyers were thoroughly after-minded. This was shown, for example, in the law of villeinage in the thirteenth century— "it seems to betray the handiwork of lawyers who have forced ancient facts into a modern theory." It was shown, too, in their attitude toward the old forms of action. As long as these were still in use it was difficult to tell the truth about their history:

> There they were, and it was the duty of judges and text writers to make the best of them, to treat them as though they formed a rational scheme provided all of a piece by some all-wise legislator. . . . It was difficult to discover, difficult to tell the truth, difficult to say that these forms of action belonged to very different ages, expressed very different and sometimes discordant theories of law, had been twisted or tortured to inappropriate uses, were the monuments of long forgotten political struggles; above all it was difficult to say of them that they had their origin and their explanation in a time when the king's court was but one among many courts.

In a recent discussion of the *quo warranto* proceedings against franchise-holders in Edward I's reign Professor Plucknett has spoken of the application of new doctrines in the interpretation of old deeds and charters by "royal lawyers who had political reasons for exaggerating their natural lack of historical sense."

Maitland's *Domesday Book and Beyond* is a conspicuous example of what he himself called the "retrogressive method" in history, the method, that is to say, of proceeding from the later known to the earlier unknown. The question may properly be asked whether this method was consistent with his teaching against after-mindedness. There was, obviously, a danger that, in using the light of Domesday Book to lighten the darkness that lay beyond, anachronism and distortion would result, that what was true of England on the day when Edward the Confessor was alive and dead would be read back too far. Maitland was alert to this danger. We have his word for it that "the method which would argue from what is in one century to what was in an earlier century, requires of him who employs it the most circumspect management." It is clear, I think, that he looked upon the retrogressive method as one to be resorted to only for want of a better, only for lack of adequate contemporary evidence. It might sometimes be necessary, but it was never for him the ideal method. It is in this sense that I read the following sentences in that trail-blazing introduction which he wrote to his edition of the roll of the Lenten Parliament of 1305:

> It is hard to think away out of our heads a history which has long lain in a remote past but which once lay in the future; it is hard to be ever remembering that such ancient terms as *house of lords* and *peers of the realm* were once new terms; it is hard to look at the thirteenth century save by looking at it through the distorting medium of the fourteenth. . . . We must judge the rolls of Edward I's reign on their own merits without reference to the parliament rolls of his grandson's, or of any later, reign.

Did Maitland, any more than his grandfather, believe that absolute historical objectivity could be attained? Some words of his in *Township and Borough* suggest an answer he might have given to this question:

If we speak, we must speak with words; if we think, we must think with thoughts. We are moderns and our words and thoughts can not but be modern. Perhaps, as Mr. Gilbert once suggested, it is too late for us to be early English. Every thought will be too sharp, every word will imply too many contrasts. We must, it is to be feared, use many words and qualify our every statement until we have almost contradicted it.

Yet Maitland never yielded to discouragement, he never became a defeatist. He was too morally wise to grow cynical about ideals because it is of their nature to be not completely attainable. He knew that a man's reach should exceed his grasp, but it never occurred to him to build a philosophy of historiography upon the difference between the two. At the end of *Domesday Book and Beyond* he concludes with a paragraph of "last words," and this paragraph concludes with these last sentences of hopeful prophecy concerning the state of materials for the knowledge of "ancient English history," and the historical sense necessary for their interpretation, at the close of the twentieth century:

Above all, by slow degrees the thoughts of our forefathers, their common thoughts about common things, will have become thinkable once more. There are discoveries to be made; but also there are habits to be formed.

A mind as acute as Maitland's was inevitably much concerned with precise meanings of words, with nice distinctions between words, with varying senses in the use of words. His sensitivity to differing shades of meaning in words is shown, for instance, by the pains he took to demonstrate that in Bracton's day the word "manor" (*manerium*) was not a technical term of law, susceptible of precise definition. As a historian of law he was impressed by the fact that lawyers had taken their terms from the popular speech and given them technical meaning and definition. Sometimes, he noted, "a word continues to have both a technical meaning for lawyers and a different and vaguer meaning for laymen." In the sixteenth century, which to Maitland's mind was so critical a period in the history of the common law, it was no small matter, it seemed to him, that English lawyers had been able to define their concepts sharply, to construct an adequate technical vocabulary, to think with precision. Technicality made the common law tough and immune to foreign legal influences. Had it been less technical and more homely, "Romanism would have swept the board in England as it swept the board in Germany."

At the very beginning of his career as a historian Maitland showed that he was already what might be called a historical semanticist, alert to changes in meaning which words have undergone in the course of time. He was ever conscious of the truth later expressed by Mr. Justice Holmes in a beautiful and famous metaphor: "A word is not a crystal, transparent and unchanged; it is the skin of a living thought and may vary greatly in color and content according to the circumstances and the time in which it is used."

Maitland's ear for gradations in the scale of meaning was extraordinarily sensitive; it would be difficult, in any of his writings, to find cases of semantic flatting or sharping. In Anglo-Saxon *diplomata* he could distinguish the tones of a whole "graduated scale of carelessness, improvement, and falsification" that lay between "unadulterated genuineness and wicked forgery." For an understanding of early English landholding much hinges, he found, upon nice distinctions between the two Latin prepositions, *sub* and *de*. "We catch a slight shade of difference between the two," he tells us in *Domesday Book and Beyond;* "*sub* lays stress on the lord's power, which may well be of a personal or justiciary, rather than of a proprietary kind, while *de* imports a theory about the origin of the tenure; it makes the tenant's rights look like derivative rights:—it is supposed that he gets his land from his lord." A vivid appreciation of the instability of meaning attached to words was one of Maitland's major historical perceptions. An instance in point was the word "landlord." "We make one word of it," he said, "and throw a strong accent on the first syllable. The lordliness has evaporated; but it was there once. Ownership has come out brightly and intensely; the element of superiority, of government, has vanished."

The problem that lies at the heart of semantics arises from the false identification of, or confusion between, the verbal labels, or *symbols,* put upon things, objects, qualities, ideas, and, in general, whatever talk or writing is about, and the things, objects, qualities, and ideas to which the symbols refer, the *referents,* as semanticists call them. In reality, of course, there is no direct and inherent connection between the verbal label and the object referred to, as Locke was at pains to point out in his *Essay concerning Human Understanding.* You are no more really ladies and gentlemen than you are *mesdames et messieurs,* and a rose by any other name would smell as sweet. But the assumption that a direct connection between symbol and referent actually exists is deeply engrained in human thinking, and semanticists regard this assumption as Public Enemy Number One. Symbols are often indeterminate and vague, and evoke widely different conceptions in different minds. Agreement regarding the referent may be called the goal of semantics.

Maitland did not employ the vocabulary of present-day semantics, which is not strange since the term itself was only beginning to come into English usage as the name of a theory, or science, of meaning toward the close of his life. But semanticists can claim him as one of theirs. Listen to this:

> When King John granted the vill of Cambridge to the burgesses and their heirs, did he mean to confer an ownership of the soil upon a municipal corporation? One point seems certain. Neither John nor his chancellor would have understood the terms of our question. Both the right that is given and the person or persons to whom it is given are hazily and feebly conceived.

Isn't Maitland telling us that King John's referents were not sharply defined in his own mind? From a modern point of view, they were vague and hazy. And if King John's thirteenth-century referents leave something to be desired from our standpoint, what can we expect of the referents of Anglo-Saxon kings in their land-books? Again let Maitland tell:

> . . . when our kings of the eighth century set their hands to documents written in Latin and bristling with the technical terms of Roman law, to documents which at first sight seem to express clear enough ideas of ownership and alienation, we must not at once assume that they have grasped these ideas.

In translating from other languages into English Maitland was confronted with the semantic problem. He frequently had to probe for an English equivalent of some foreign word and could not always find it. It was often difficult, if not impossible, he discovered, to translate a medieval Latin word accurately, and sometimes he had to be satisfied with the least inadequate English rendering of a German expression. He came to the conclusion that an English translation of the work of a German lawyer could, at best, never be entirely satisfactory: "To take the most obvious instance, his *Recht* is never quite our *Right* or quite our *Law*." Sometimes a German word seemed to Maitland definitely preferable to its not quite equivalent English translation. He was led to speculate on the comparative semantic merits of the English and German languages for legal history. The German historian, he concluded, had at his disposal more accurate terms and concepts than his English counterpart, but this was not an unmitigated advantage for it might lead him to construct theories about early times too sharp to be true. Still he could see possibilities, said Maitland, that are "concealed from us in our fluffier language; and the sharp onesided theory will at least state the problem that is to be solved."

Maitland's writings—his books, articles, introductions, and reviews—come to us from the generation before last, and it should go without saying that they are not at all points fully abreast of today's scholarship. Some of his opinions have been questioned, and here and there they have been corrected. To demonstrate this specifically would serve no present purpose, even if the hour were earlier. It should be said, however, that this is how he would have had it, for nothing was nearer to his heart than the hope that the work which was so dear to him would be carried forward by others, and he was, as we have seen, a welling source of inspiration. We may say of him what he said of an English historian of the generation before his own, J. M. Kemble—that no one "who has felt the difference between genius and industrious good intentions" can ever differ with him lightly or without regret. It is significant that Maitland's principal critics have been among his warmest admirers.

Judged, as every scholar ought to be judged, in relation to the state of knowledge and the standards of learning of his own day, Maitland was a towering figure. In an obituary article on his old friend and collaborator, Sir Frederick Pollock wrote:

> It is not easy to convey an adequate notion of Maitland's work to those who have not themselves labored in the same field. It is still less easy for any one to appreciate the difficulties or the success who does not remember the conditions under which he started. . . . Looking back some twenty-five years, we see the early history of the Common Law still obscure, insulated, a seeming chaos of technical antiquities. Historians excusably shrank from it, and the lawyers who really knew much of it could almost be counted on one's fingers. . . . This was the world which Maitland's genius transformed. . . . So complete has the transformation been that our children will hardly believe how uncritical their grandfathers were, and on what palpable fictions they were nourished. . . . Maitland commanded the dry bones to live, and henceforth they are alive.

And one final estimate, by Sir William Holdsworth, the historian of English law, who was proud to profess himself a disciple of Maitland: "In an age of great historians I think that Maitland was the greatest, I think that he was the equal of the greatest lawyers of his day, and that, as a legal historian, English law from before the time of legal memory has never known his like."

ROBERT LIVINGSTON SCHUYLER

A Historical Sketch of Liberty and Equality

AS IDEALS OF ENGLISH POLITICAL PHILOSOPHY FROM THE TIME OF HOBBES TO THE TIME OF COLERIDGE

Liberty

The simplest meaning of the word "Liberty" is absence of restraint. To the political philosopher it means absence of restraint on human action, and, since we are not speaking of the metaphysical freedom of the will, we may say absence of external restraint on human action. Further, as politicians, we are not concerned with those restraints which are due to causes over which we have no control; we have only to deal with those external restraints on human action which are themselves the results of human action. But we cannot say that the Liberty which our philosophers praise is an absence of *all* such re-

Submitted as a dissertation for a Fellowship at Trinity and privately printed in 1875.

straints: the minimization of all restraints on human action is an ideal of politics which has but lately made its appearance. No, the Liberty which our earlier philosophers praise is—

(1) The absence of restraints imposed by certain persons;

or   (2) The absence of certain forms of restraint;

or   (3) The absence of restraints on certain classes of actions.

To examine at some length the history of Liberty as a political ideal is the object of this present chapter.

Naturally enough, the political question which most attracted philosophers in the seventeenth century was the question: How can one man or body of men obtain a rightful title to rule other men? The great demand for political theory produced a somewhat injurious effect on the supply. Coleridge has remarked how, in times of great political excitement, the terms in which political theories are expressed become, not more and more practical, but more and more abstract and unpractical. It is in such times that men clothe their theories in universal terms, and preface their creeds by the widest of propositions. The absolute spirit is abroad. Relative or partial good seems a poor ideal; it is not of these, or those men that we speak, of this nation, or that age, but of Man. Philosophers in the seventeenth century were not content with shewing that this or that government would be the best for our nation, that it would make Englishmen good, or virtuous, or happy; they sought to strengthen their position by shewing that some form of government is universally and eternally the only right one. God and Nature, said the friends of the Stuarts, have decreed that we should submit to an absolute monarch. God and Nature, replied their opponents, have decreed that the consent of the governed can alone give a title to the governor. Both parties tried to answer the question as to what is the right form of government, without first answering more fundamental questions. They did, of course, occasionally refer to some standard, such as the good or welfare of the community; but their main effort was to transcend such considerations, and to give a summary decision as to the right form of government, without first considering the end for which all government should exist. They did not wish to compare, as Aristotle had done, the good and evil of various polities, but rather to shew that such a comparison is unnecessary. Such a procedure was unphilosophical. It is not possible to decide who ought to govern until we know what a government ought to do. By reversing the natural order of these questions political philosophy involved itself in a maze of fictions.

These fictions were introduced as substitutes for an answer to the question: What is it that governments ought to do? They were really ethical doctrines disguised as pieces of history. This mixture of ethics and history was very disastrous. When the limits of the royal power are under discussion, it is often hard to say whether the question is as to the limits which *have been* placed to the royal power, or as to the limits which *ought to be* placed to the royal power. In fact we can distinguish no less than four questions as involved, viz.: What limits do (1) positive law, (2) positive morality, (3) ideal law, (4) ideal morality, set to the royal power? At the present day it would be easy to distinguish these. We can say what power law and opinion allow to the king, without trespassing on the realm of what ought to be. But in the seventeenth century this was harder to do, for several reasons—

(1) The constitution of this country was not nearly so well defined as it now is; there were gaps in it—points on which there was no case to appeal to. The question, "Who is sover-

eign?" could scarcely be answered, the fact being that some-times the king, sometimes the king and Parliament had be-haved as sovereign, and been acknowledged as such.

(2) The confusion as to who was sovereign was increased by that curious doctrine of our Constitution which was being slowly formulated, namely, that though the king is subject to no law, he cannot absolve any other person from the laws made by king and Parliament; that royal immunity is coupled with ministerial responsibility.

(3) The legal fiction of the perfection of the English Com-mon Law, the supposition that there is somewhere a code of perfect law, by means of which an English judge may supple-ment the statutes (though at one stage of our progress necessary for the administration of substantial justice), produced injuri-ous effects on political theory. Controversialists could so easily pass from the existing law to that law of perfect reason to which our judges appealed when in want of a new principle. This should be remembered when we hear Austin talking of "jargon" and "fustian." It may now be inexcusable to confuse law as it ought to be with law as it is, the ideal with the positive; but in the seventeenth century it was almost impossible to draw this line, for the ideal was constantly becoming the positive. Our judges were obliged to introduce new principles, and were obliged to introduce them *as if they were parts of a pre-existing law.*

In all these ways ethics were mixed with history, the ideal with the positive, until it is difficult to see how far an author is describing what is, how far he is giving an opinion as to what ought to be.

The main question which the philosophers of the seven-teenth century had to answer was, How can one man, or body of men, acquire an authority over others which these latter ought to obey, and ought to be made to obey? The answers which were given to this question were two. (1) God (or nature) has given to some men a title to rule, independent of all consent. (2) A title to rule can only be acquired by consent. These answers took many different forms, and sometimes we find intermediate theories, but the twofold division must serve our present purpose. These two theories of the rightful title to rule we may call *the natural* and *the conventional*.

I. Those who asserted that some men have a title to rule others, which does not depend upon consent, were frequent in their appeals to Aristotle. Aristotle was, for many reasons, the most popular of the classical writers on politics. In no department of philosophy, except perhaps that of deductive logic, has the influence of Aristotle been so long and so strongly felt as in that of politics. No history of the British Constitution would be complete which did not point out how much its growth has been affected by ideas derived from Aristotle. The common sayings about the excellence of a mixture of the simple forms of government, about subjecting the rulers to the laws, have an Aristotelian as well as an empirical origin, and accepted commonplaces are powerful agents in moulding a constitution. We cannot indeed ascribe any one very definite tendency to Aristotle's influence, for his Politics are singularly undogmatic; but his disinterested curiosity discovered many-sided truths, some portions of which every school of political philosophers has been willing to accept. On this very question of the title to rule he could not fairly be appealed to by any of our seventeenth century controversialists, save perhaps Algernon Sydney. It is true that Aristotle held that some men have a title to rule others even when the consent of the latter has not been asked, but his idea of a natural title to rule scarcely suited the Caroline divines and lawyers. The classical, ideal polity, whether as conceived by Aristotle or as conceived by Plato, is an aristocracy, or monarchy of merit. The test of a man's natural title to rule is the possession of the power and will to rule well. No other test of a natural title was (as far as I know) ever dreamt of by a Greek philosopher. Now Sir Robert Filmer and his friends were glad enough to find Aristotle maintaining that some men are born to rule, and others to serve; but this doctrine has its dangerous side—it leads to such speculations as those of Sydney, about the right of the virtuous man to rule. What Filmer and his colleagues had to justify was the feudal notion of hereditary right. A justification of feudalism was not to be obtained from Aristotle, so they turned to the other great source of authority—the Bible.

It was said that God has given the sovereignty of the whole world to Adam and his heirs (or heirs males) for ever; that the heir of Adam, or failing him, the heir of the last person who filled the place of Adam's heir, is rightfully king. This is as accurate a statement as I can make of a theory which, though legal in its pretensions, was never stated with legal accuracy. With this was combined the theory that civil power is in its origin paternal or patriarchal power. Now, as far as history is concerned, the Divine Right School were nearer the truth than their opponents. Modern writers have taught us that the first rulers are fathers of families, that the fiction of relationship between the governors and the governed is kept up long after the fact has ceased, and that, on the death of the father of the family, common consent allows his power to devolve upon his eldest son. The Bible supplied these facts, and was supposed to supply them as precedents. But much more than this was

wanted. It was necessary to shew that God has decreed that
the power of a dead monarch shall devolve according to certain
ascertainable canons of inheritance; to shew (*e.g.*) that the Salic
law is or is not such a canon, or that it is so in France, but not
in England. It is needless to say that nothing of the sort could
be done. The law which regulates the Royal Succession in England is only a law of God, if the whole of our common and
statute law is a law of God. It is not even a part of *Jus Gentium*,
the law common to all nations. Every Christian, it is true, looks
upon his duties as divinely appointed; obedience to rulers is,
within certain limits, a duty, and, a Christian would say, a duty
set us by God; but this does not imply that God has singled out
this or that man to rule, unless we use the words in a sense
which makes every event, good or bad, the result of Divine will.
The appeal to the Bible was singularly unfortunate. The Old
Testament is the history of a nation which sinned in asking for
a king, and which more than once interfered with the hereditary succession of the royal line. Many Puritans believed that
they had precisely the same justification for killing Charles that
Jehu had for killing Ahab. The New Testament contains many
commands of obedience to *de facto* governments, not one rule
for selecting a sovereign *de jure;* it is the powers that be, not the
powers that ought to be, that we are to obey; indeed, quotations
from the New Testament come better from Hobbes, the supporter of *de facto* governments, than from the preachers of the
Divine right of hereditary monarchy. It is almost impossible to
believe that some of the arguments drawn from Scripture by
the friends of the Stuarts were put forward in good faith. In the
whole history of delusion there is nothing stranger than the
claim of sovereignty for Adam's heir. Many people seem to
think that this claim was a fiction of Whigs like Locke, got up

to discredit the Tories; but as a fact we find the argument repeated by writer after writer of undoubted probity. Failing the support of the Scriptures, there was nothing for the theory to rest on save expedience, and this was too low a ground for the preachers of Divine right. No one (as far as I know) has asserted that we perceive intuitively that hereditary monarchy is at all times, and in all places, the one right form of government. The nearest approach to such an assertion that I can find is in the *Jus Regium* of Sir George Mackenzie, a reply to Buchanan's *De Jure Regni*, where it is said that hereditary succession is according to the law of nature; but, after all, the law of nature appears only to give us the truism that in a *hereditary* monarchy the *heir* should succeed.[1] This book of Mackenzie's, for which he received the thanks of the University of Oxford, is a most extraordinary display of the weakness of the Divine Right School, and makes the grave faults of Locke's works seem venial. If the purely Scriptural argument fails, then the whole question of the best form of government is again thrown open. If its defenders cannot shew that hereditary monarchy has been expressly commanded by God, they may be required to shew that it answers to some standard of political good, that it would make a nation moral or happy.

We may notice two forms of the theory: the stricter, which, giving to Adam absolute power, did not admit that any part of this had been alienated by him or his successors; and the milder, which allowed that successive kings had granted away portions of the originally complete power which could not be resumed by themselves or their successors. The first form was advocated by Filmer, the second by Clarendon.

---

1. *Mackenzie's Works*, vol. II. p. 472.

Filmer was an acute controversialist, and hit both Hobbes and Milton some hard blows. But even he is obliged to admit that a prince is bound by his "own just and reasonable conventions"; the prince however being the judge of their justice.[2] This concession renders his apology for absolute monarchy weaker than that of Hobbes, who, by making the prince the fountain of morality as well as of law, sought to deprive the subjects of any ground from which they might criticise the prince's acts.

The more moderate believers in Divine hereditary right found a spokesman in Clarendon. Filmer had read the *De Cive* "with no small content,"[3] Clarendon had never read a "book containing so much sedition, treason, and impiety as this *Leviathan.*"[4] Like Roger Coke, and others, he thought that Hobbes had damaged the king's cause. The king, he held, had been invested by God and Nature with complete power, but some of this had been irrevocably granted away by charters, and so forth; he speaks of monarchical power as a trust, and holds the king bound by his own and his ancestors' promises.[5] Sir George Mackenzie made a similar damaging admission; he goes further; the king may not interfere with the rights of property.[6] Now this is to surrender the stronghold of Divine right. If power be a trust, if it be possible to diminish it by grant, we must, as Hobbes knew well, retire from the high ground of natural right to the low ground of advisability. For the question arises—Is *cestui que trust* to have no remedy against his trustee

---

2. *The Power of Kings*, etc.
3. *Observations on Aristotle's Politics*, etc.
4. *A Brief View . . . the Leviathan*, p. 319.
5. Ibid., pp. 72, 122.
6. Ibid., vol. II. p. 451.

in case of a breach of trust? What if the king attempt to regain his surrendered rights? Thus unless we can accept the strictest form of the theory, and go beyond Filmer himself in freeing kings from all their promises, the question is again thrown open. Though God may have given the sovereignty upon trust to Adam and his heirs, may they not forfeit it? Clarendon's book was really a heavy blow to the straiter sect of the Divine Right School, for he brings into prominence the discrepancies between Hobbism and common sense, and Hobbes' conclusions, though not his premises, were dear to the most thorough of the monarchical party. In many respects it is a very just criticism of Hobbes, it is the protest of a historian against Hobbes' practice of deciding historical and constitutional questions "by speculation and deduction," from psychological generalities. It is like Macaulay's protest against James Mill's Essay.

Mediaeval feudalism masquerading in a Hebrew dress was a strange apparition. Of such a fiction as the original contract we may say it was never invented, it grew; but somebody must have invented this claim for Adam's heir—and to whom the honour belongs I cannot say. There seems no evidence of its having been put forward prior to the accession of the Stuarts, and it appears to be of English origin. In the *Political Discourses* of James Tyrrell, a book in which the rival theories of government are discussed with much moderation, it is not suggested that any early ecclesiastical authority could be found for this doctrine. It disappeared as suddenly as it appeared. Sydney and Locke exposed the ineptitudes of Filmer's Old Testament history so thoroughly, that the work has never wanted doing again. But their arguments were powerfully backed up by the conduct of the clergy. Hobbes had seen that the alliance between the Church and absolute monarchy was accidental, and tried to justify the latter on non-religious as well as religious grounds. The clergy had made a large mental reservation when preaching the Divine right of kings, as was shewn when they refused to read the Declaration.

But below the talk about Adam's heir there lay a just protest against the theory, then rising into power, which admits of no title to rule, but a title by consent. This, which I call the conventional theory, did not fairly start on its course until the time of Locke, but we see it in Hooker, Milton, and Sydney, struggling with the theory that some men have a title to rule others without first obtaining their consent—that we have a duty to obey governments to which we have not consented. This theory of a natural title to rule had been mixed with the absurdities of Filmer, Heylin, and Mackenzie, and fell into bad repute; but we find it rising again in Hume, who does not require the consent of the governed in order to make government just. The utilitarian may have to admit a title to rule not derived from consent; and though for a moment the results of utilitarianism and of the conventional theory appeared to coincide when James Mill and Bentham put forward "the junction-of-interests principle," as a deduction from "the greater happiness principle," they have since fallen asunder, and will not again be easily united. But of this more hereafter.

II. We must now pass to the conventional theory of government, having described the antagonist with which, at the outset, it had to contend. Filmer and Clarendon did not admit that Liberty was on their opponents' side, but it must be allowed that there is nothing in the bare idea of a government *not* based upon consent that can be said to answer to our idea of freedom; the upholders of the conventional theory can much more speciously claim that the government which they would establish is "a free government."

Filmer and his friends might protest, with what truth remains to be seen, that the conventional theory leads not to Liberty but to license, but this theory has been generally known as the theory of Civil Liberty. It might be expressed thus— Men have a right to be under no government save that to which they have consented. Government ought to be founded on agreement or contract. A word as to its origin—Christian theology contemplated the relations which exist between the Supreme Ruler and his subjects as partly dependent on a covenant, and it was natural (though not necessarily logical) that these should be taken as types of the relations which ought to exist between an earthly ruler and his subjects. Again, laws first appear in the history of mankind as the formulation of already existing customs, and not as the expression of the will of a superior. Hence the essential distinction between an agreement and a law is one which is slowly evolved, and we see that by some of our earlier philosophers a law was still looked upon as obtaining its binding force by being the outcome of a contract. We may add that the histories of Greece and Rome dazzled the eyes of those to whom the new learning was opened. From them, more especially from the history of Rome, men learnt to look upon the right to a share in the government (the right of self-government) as one of the privileges of a citizen, forgetting probably how small a portion of the inhabitants of Rome were citizens.

We may also remark that throughout the history of English ethics there runs a tendency to resolve all duties into the duties of speaking the truth, and of fulfilling contracts. It has been thought that there is a peculiar irrationality in letting our deeds and words contradict each other. Even Hobbes occasionally falls into this strain of language,[7] an inconsistency which did

7. *Works* (ed. Molesworth), III. 119.

not escape the eye of Clarke.[8] The "rational" moralists, looking at a right action as a recognition of a proportion or fitness, were naturally led to identify right action and true affirmation. This tendency to resolve all duties into truthfulness and fidelity is observable in the attempt to ground all our duties to God on a solemn league and covenant, and in the attempt to base all our political duties on some agreement or contract. Perhaps the reason for this is, that "Speak truth" and "Keep promises" are supposed to admit of fewer exceptions than do other ethical maxims.

At any rate the theory that sovereignty ought to be founded on consent is laid down with great distinctness by Hooker, who contrasts it with the doctrine of Aristotle. He says that men knew that "strifes and troubles would be endless, except they gave their common consent all to be ordered by some whom they should agree upon: without which consent there was no reason that one man should take upon him to be lord, or judge over another; because, although there be according to the opinion of some very great and judicious men, a kind of natural right in the noble, and wise, and virtuous, to govern them which are of servile disposition; nevertheless, for manifestation of their right, and men's more peaceable contentment on both sides, the assent of them who are governed seemeth necessary."[9] Here we see the two theories lying side by side, and Hooker, in making his choice of that which requires the consent of the governed, was doing what was of more importance to the world than he can have been aware of. This theory passed from Hooker to Locke, from Locke to Rousseau, and has profoundly affected the history of mankind. For some time after its appear-

8. *Evidences*, etc. (ed. 1728), p. 178.
9. *Eccl. Pol.* I. x.

ance it remained comparatively powerless, for it was coupled with no very definite principle laying down whose consent it is that we must require, or what is to be considered evidence of such consent. It did not become really active until it was allied with the doctrine that all men are equal, and that therefore when the governed give their consent every man is to count for one. The alliance was not firmly established until the time of Locke; but long before this there is observable a tendency, especially among the Puritans, to look upon all men as equal, a tendency which had its origin in Christianity itself. Though submission to the powers that be is a cardinal virtue in the Christian scheme, and though it would be even harder to find the conventional than to find the hereditary theory of government in the Bible, there is in the Christian idea of all men as equal in the sight of Omniscience, a germ of that doctrine of natural equality which was required in order to give definiteness to the conventional theory. δῆμος μὲν γὰρ ἐγένετο ἐκ τοῦ ἴσους ὁτιοῦν ὄντας οἴεσθαι ἁπλῶς ἴσους εἶναι.[10] But the idea of Christian equality was not definite enough; and we do not find that Puritans, such as Milton, accepted that equality of faculties which is the starting point of Locke's system.

The difficulty of reconciling the natural and conventional theories of authority is forced upon us in reading Milton's political works. For, on the one hand, he held that all sovereignty is from the people; on the other hand, he was far from accepting the democratic ideal, that in matters of government every man should have one vote, and that a majority must decide. He justifies the action of the army in interfering with the Parliament.

10. [For Democracy arose from men's thinking that, if they were equal in some respect, then they were equal in every respect.] Arist. *Pol.* v. i.

"The soldiers judged better than the Great Council, and by arms saved the Commonwealth, which the Great Council had almost damned by their votes."[11] Indeed, it is difficult to see how Cromwell's proceedings could be justified by one who held that all government ought to rest upon the consent of the people. Filmer points out this difficulty forcibly, and justly. Here we see, he argues, what these Puritans mean by "the People," it is "the best principled" part, and the Army is the sole judge of good principles.[12] It is impossible to reconcile the Puritan ideal of a reign of the Saints with the ideal of a Government founded on consent; the Saints were to reign whether sinners liked it or not. If our great dogma that government ought to rest on consent be to differ from "the simple rule . . . the good old plan," the consent required must be more than a mere absence of resistance; and if we require more than this, Cromwell had as little title by consent as had Charles. How little Milton cared for the popular voice may be seen in his letter to Monk written just before the Restoration. He wishes that good republicans should be returned to Parliament, and if the people "refuse these fair and noble offers of an immediate Liberty," then Monk is to use his "faithful veteran army." And this is called "A ready and easy way to establish a free Government." A ready and easy way no doubt, but in what sense would a Government established by a military *coup d'état* be "free"? But sometimes Milton throws aside the pretence of founding government upon the consent of the people. "More just it is doubtless, if it come to force, that a less number compel a greater to retain what can be no wrong to them, their liberty,

11. *Defence . . . against Salmasius.*
12. *Observations,* etc.

than that a greater number, for the pleasure of their baseness, compel a less most injuriously to be their fellow slaves."[13] Here the conventional theory is thrown aside; those who can, and will preserve liberty (*i.e.,* a popular form of government), have a natural title to rule. Milton was in a great strait, for it was becoming evident that if the people agreed upon any government, it would be government by their old tyrants.

The same difficulty occurs in Algernon Sydney's *Discourses Concerning Government.* The title by nature is not here the Puritan title of God's elect, but the philosophic title of the wise and virtuous man. Sydney often insists on the natural inequality of men. "That equality which is just among equals is just only among equals; but such as are base, ignorant, vicious, slothful, or cowardly, are not equal in natural or acquired virtues to the generous, wise, valiant, and industrious; nor equally useful to the societies in which they live; they cannot therefore have an equal part in the government of them; they cannot equally provide for the common good; and it is not a personal but a public benefit that is sought in their constitution and continuance. . . . If the nature of man be reason, 'detur digniori,' in matters of this kind, is the voice of nature."[14] Here is the natural theory, but when we turn to Sydney's definition of liberty we find: "I desire it may not be forgotten, that the liberty asserted is not a licentiousness of doing what is pleasing to every one against the command of God, but an exemption from all human laws, to which they have not given their assent."[15] Here is a particularly strong statement of the conventional theory, it

13. *A Ready and Easy Way,* etc.
14. *Discourses,* ch. ii. § i.
15. *Discourses,* ch. i. § ii.

is stronger than Locke's definition. "The liberty of man in society is to be under no other legislative power, but that established by consent in the Commonwealth; nor under the dominion of any will, or restraint of any law, but what the legislative shall enact according to the trust put in it."[16] Sydney requires the assent of the people *to the laws,* Locke requires that the government established shall have been consented to, and shall legislate according to certain rules which have also been consented to. But though Sydney uses this very strong expression, an expression which at once identifies Civil Liberty and Democracy, this is not his usual language. He would, I think, have been content if the legislative body were elected by the people, or even if the outlines of government were consented to by the people. But even this requirement of popular consent is scarcely to be harmonized with the "detur digniori" which he elsewhere makes his motto.

Locke and Sydney speak as if civil governments ought to be based on consent, and they also assert that good governments have as a fact been the result of an agreement between the rulers and the ruled. Hobbes also makes his Commonwealth rest upon a covenant. We may ask how far these authors supposed that governments have been the result of agreement, how far the original contract was for them a fact? Here we must draw a distinction. Hobbes, the defender of established governments, speaks very positively about a contract being the foundation of all dominion, but he does not make it clear whether this contract was made once for all, or whether it is renewed by each generation of citizens. He knows nothing of a tacit contract, nor does he speak as if the contract was made for self and pos-

16. *Essays on Government,* II. 22.

terity, or for self, heirs, and assigns in respect of property possessed. He always speaks as if every citizen covenanted for himself, and for himself only. But at the same time he speaks as if the social contract had been made once for all. I do not think that Hobbes believed that any such contract has really been made; he looked upon the conventional theory as an apt fiction, expressing the duties of governors and governed. But with Sydney and Locke the case was different, they really thought that all rightful government had been the result of an agreement between the rulers and the ruled; they did not for one moment admit that the conventional theory was only a convenient fiction; they maintained that where there had been good government, that government was the result of a social contract, and that no government could be good which did not rest on such a contract.

Now, as a piece of history, the conventional theory has no foundation, and is far inferior to the patriarchal theory. Not one single instance of a covenant by a whole nation, or even by that part of a nation which is not under what may be called natural disabilities, can be produced. It is not until a late period in the history of men that the idea of settling their social relations by contract arises. The constitutions of the American States cannot be appealed to in support of the historical truth of the theory, for they were the results of a belief in the theory.

Clarendon and Filmer triumphantly ask for one solitary example of a social contract, and Sydney and Locke did try hard to produce one. Sydney promises to prove that these contracts are historical facts, "real, solemn and obligatory." But it is not unworthy of remark that this promise is followed by a hiatus in his manuscript, and is never fulfilled.[17] Locke again tries to find

17. *Discourses*, II. xxxii.

an answer, but is compelled to content himself for the most part with saying that there is no evidence to the contrary.[18] Elsewhere he admits the patriarchal origin of Government.[19] Then he argues for the probability *à priori* of there having been a social contract,[20] and finally he changes his ground, the compact was not made once for all when men left the state of nature, but is made by every citizen.[21]

But on the whole, though Milton and Sydney admit the conventional theory to be true, and sometimes state it in strong terms, their use of it is not so much constructive as destructive. They appeal to it in order to put the Divine Right School out of court, and, when this is done, they fall back upon the natural inequality of men; the Saints, those who would "reform the Reformation," or the wise and virtuous have a natural title to rule, and it is hard to see how they would reconcile this with that conventional theory which only gained its full strength when Locke, following Hobbes, preached that men are by nature equal.

Here, in a sort of parenthesis, we may notice one of the greatest of our great Commonwealthsmen. Harrington was one of the first to oppose Hobbes on what would now be called utilitarian grounds. Accepting Hobbes' identification of reason and interest, he decides that it is not the interest of the individual, but the interest of mankind, which is Right Reason.[22] The argument is rather fanciful, and assumes that the different parts of inanimate nature fly to each other's assistance, so that the

---

18. *Gov.* II. 101.
19. Ibid., II. 76.
20. Ibid., II. 112.
21. Ibid., II. 117.
22. *Harrington's Works* (ed. Toland), p. 44.

whole may be perfect; and man, he thinks, must not be "less just than the creature." "Now compute well," he says, "for if the interest of popular government come the nearest to the interest of mankind, then the reason of popular government must be the nearest to Right Reason." This he decides, by rather inconclusive reasoning, must be the case. Democracy, moderated by allowing to an aristocracy the power of proposing, though not of making laws, is the best form of government. He is far from having arrived at Locke's point of view, and will do all he can to give authority to the best and wisest. He does not ignore good birth and good breeding as qualifications for power. "For so it is in the universal series of story, that if any man founded a Commonwealth he was first a gentleman," his examples include Moses, Romulus, and others.[23] However, the people or their representatives ought to have the power of making laws.

Harrington is a very interesting figure in the history of political philosophy. At a time when Hobbes would content himself with nothing under a universal proposition, a proposition applicable, not to these or those men, but to Man, Harrington saw the importance of consulting the history of that nation for which we are setting up an ideal. Again, he saw how few political ideals are realizable, and while his contemporaries were talking as if we had only to choose the best form of government, and then to try and establish it by direct means, Harrington decided that as long as the distribution of property remains constant, only one form of government is possible; the balance of power depends on the balance of property.[24] Most certainly this is not a complete analysis of the positive conditions which make the establishment of a government possible, and Hume's

23. Ibid., p. 56.
24. Ibid., pp. 40 *et seq.*

criticisms on Harrington are just,[25] but it was a step in the right direction, and Hume recognized it as such. In fact Harrington is particularly interesting because he would seem to have exercised a considerable influence on Hume. Hume says that the Oceana "is the only valuable model of a Commonwealth that has yet been offered to the public,"[26] and, even remembering Plato's great work, there is much truth in this praise; for Harrington tried always to remember that an ideal which requires an essential alteration in the nature of man has but little value.

Something must here be said of Hobbes' apology for *de facto* governments and existing laws, an apology which is the centre of his philosophy. In Hobbes' day such an apology was by no means unnecessary. Puritanism asserting the claims of conscience and the rights of private judgment, had rushed into a sort of anti-nomianism. No laws were to be obeyed which did not come up to some standard of ideal justice. It must be doubtful which is the greatest error in theory, the assertion of Hobbes that positive laws are the measure of justice, or the Puritan doctrine that laws which are not good are not to be obeyed, though there can be little doubt that the latter is the more dangerous. The Puritans set up an ideal law of God, discoverable partly by study of the Scriptures, partly by the light of reason, and positive laws which did not agree with this law of God were looked upon as void.

The jural conception of morality has always been common; if we do not find it in Greek philosophy, we at least find it in Greek poetry.[27] With the Bible before him, this is the conception most natural to the Christian. Now, if we take the jural

---

25. *Hume's Essays*, I. vii.

26. Ibid., II. xvi.

27. Soph. *Antig.* vv. 445 *et seq.*

view of morality, there appears more probability of a conflict between civil law and morality than if we take an aesthetic view. But this was not all. "*Jus Naturae*" had meant much more than is meant by our expression "the moral law." The idea of *Jus Naturae* sprang from the *Jus Gentium* of Rome, when brought into contact with the later Stoic philosophy. *Jus Gentium* was the law administered to strangers at Rome, a law drawn from the observances common to those nations to which the strangers belonged. A law which is found in all communities may be looked upon as natural; the laws of this or that state may be due to caprice, to casual local circumstances, in a word, they are artificial; but a law which is found in all states must be due to the very nature of man. Having gone thus far, it is easy to look upon *Jus Gentium* as more truly a Divine law than the laws of any one state can be. It is the result of man's nature as God made it. And thus we pass from *Jus Gentium*, a real positive law—just as positive as the maxims of our modern Court of Chancery—to the *Jus Naturae*, a Divine law, to which all civil law *ought*, at least in its outlines, to conform. In a word, the law of nature comes to mean ideal law—law as it ought to be. But another change lay before it. By the time of which we are speaking, the idea of *Jus Gentium* is fast fading away; scarcely a trace of it remains in Grotius' celebrated definition; the law of nature is fast becoming a synonym for the moral law, *i.e.,* a code of ideal morality. The law of nature of Butler's Sermons is no longer even ideal law; it is ideal morality. But among the political writers of whom we are speaking, "the law of nature" retained some of its old force—it still meant something more legal and more "positive" than our "morality." The law of nature might still be appealed to in our courts of justice as supplementing and even overriding the statutes of the realm. The courts, particularly the Court of Chancery, were by no means averse to administering what passed as "natural law." Under this disguise they frequently introduced their new principles. The fiction "aequitas est perfecta quaedam ratio, quae jus scriptum interpretatur *et emendat*" was still kept up, and this *perfecta ratio* was a faculty discovering the law of nature. It is not uninteresting to notice that Cumberland dedicates his book *De Legibus Naturae*—a work on what we should call morality—to the Chancellor, as the proper custodian of the law of nature, so fused were the ideas of law and morality in the idea of natural law. Thus the law of nature was sometimes an ideal for the law maker, sometimes an ideal for the moralist, sometimes an ideal for the law administrator, the judge. Between these different meanings it was easy to flit, and confusion was the result.

This conception of natural law led to a disrespect of positive law, to that sort of anti-nomianism which we find in Milton's works. Milton defended the regicides against Salmasius by saying that the king's execution was *legal,* it was according to the law of God, Reason, and Nature. If a statute can be produced giving tyrannical power to a king, this being contrary to God's will, to Reason, and to Nature, "is not of force with us." It will be observed that he does not say that if the king's execution be contrary to the positive law of the land it is *illegal,* but at the same time it is *morally good.* No, he says, though it be opposed to our statutes it is *legal,* for it is according to the law of God; thus it is just as *legal* as the execution of a murderer under our common law. And Milton could justify himself by appealing to the procedure of law courts which daily professed to administer the law of nature. Sydney, again, heads a chapter with the startling statement "that which is not just is not law, and that which is not law ought not to be obeyed."[28] Milton and Sydney would

28. *Discourses,* etc., III. xi.

probably not have said that we can never have a duty to obey positive law as positive law, that we can never have a duty to obey positive law when it commands some action which, were it not for that law, would be bad, but they habitually use language placing no limit to our duty of disobeying unjust laws. All men, when not engaged in controversy, would probably say that the truth lies between Hobbes and Milton, that the mere fact that positive law commands an action is *some* reason why we should do it; that we have a duty to obey the law of the land because it is the law of the land; but that this duty may conflict with other duties, and in such cases we must appeal to some higher rule of ethics. To the utilitarian this is obvious, and most non-utilitarian moralists would admit a special duty of Order or Obedience to Law. Thus we cannot say with Hobbes that we never have a duty to disobey positive law, nor with the Puritans that positive law cannot make it our duty to do what, in the absence of positive law, would have been indifferent, or even bad.

It has scarcely been sufficiently noticed that Hobbes was, to some extent, an eclectic in politics. The premises are the premises of Sydney and Locke, but the conclusion is the conclusion of Filmer. He justifies absolute monarchy by referring, not to the natural inequality of men, but to their natural equality. He will not say with Aristotle that some men are made to rule, others to serve, for this is contrary to both reason and experience.[29] He knew well that the arguments of the Divine Right School would never stand examination, and he conceived the grand idea of basing politics on a true system of ethics, which should itself rest on a true psychology. He grants to the Common-

29. *Hobbes' English Works* (ed. Molesworth), vol. III. 140, 141.

wealthsman all that he seems to require. Men are born with equal faculties; they are born free; all government ought to rest upon consent. But he attempts to turn the ideas of natural liberty and natural equality into a defence of *de facto* governments. He does not succeed in this, for the social covenant on which he allows government to rest is obviously a mere fiction, and he would have found it hard to answer the Commonwealthsman who said, "You admit that I was born free, and that I have a natural right to be under no government save that to which I have consented. Now I affirm that I have not consented to King Charles' government." If I understand Hobbes aright, he meant that the mere fact of the existence of a government must be taken as conclusive evidence of the consent to it of all those who enjoy its protection, all express declarations to the contrary notwithstanding, and that men are morally and religiously bound by their supposed consent. But such a theory is very unstable, the premises are the legitimate property of the democrat, not of the apologist for *de facto* governments. If it be allowed that all men are naturally free and equal, if all rightful government is founded on consent, men will not be put off with a fictitious consent; they will say, "You admit that consent is necessary, a *fictitious* consent cannot be necessary, the necessary consent must be real."

Undoubtedly the main doctrine of Hobbes' politics is that we ought always to obey the existing government, and our duty of obedience arises from the fact, or rather the fiction, that we have covenanted with our fellows to do so. This being so, we should naturally expect that Hobbes had some peculiar notion of the superior obligation of the duty of fidelity when compared with other duties. But we find that it is only self-love, or rather a desire for self-preservation, which obliges us to enter into the social covenant, and abide by it when made. He has to shew that prudence, or the desire for a tolerable life, counsels us to surrender our natural right to all things, hand it over to some sovereign, one or many, and abstain from all attempts to resume it. Hallam thinks Hobbes' assertion, that all men have by nature equal capacities, not requisite to his theory.[30] To me it appears not only requisite, but absolutely necessary. Hobbes' chief concern is to prove that men are equal *in their power of hurting others,* so that he may shew that it is to the advantage not only of the weak but also of the strong to enter civil society. "They are equals," he says, "who can do equal things one against the other; but they who can do the greatest thing, namely, kill, can do equal things. All men among themselves are by nature equal."[31] He certainly does go further than this, and affirms that all men are equal in their mental faculties, but this also was necessary, for it was incumbent on him to get rid of the Aristotelian natural title to rule. What however concerns him most is to shew that no man is so strong in body or mind that it will profit him to remain in the state of nature. He ought however to prove not only that every man will find it profitable to enter the civil state, but also that prudence, or the desire of self-preservation, counsels us to refrain from occasional backslidings towards the state of nature. This is one of his attempts at proof. Men, he says, are so equal in their power of hurting each other that it will not profit any man, however strong in body or mind, to remain in or return to the state of nature. But to this he adds a consideration which is rather out of place in his system. There would be a sort of absurdity in breaking our cove-

---

30. *Hist. Lit.,* vol. II., p. 538.
31. *Hobbes' English Works,* vol. II. 7.

nants, a sort of self-contradiction.[32] He does not however make it clear that prudence, or the desire for self-preservation, can never counsel us to contradict ourselves; and this he was bound to do.

Thus, instead of giving us peculiarly strong reasons for keeping our covenants, he gives us very weak reasons, for it is far from being self-evident that we can never be gainers by a breach of the laws. The absurdity of basing an absolute and indefeasible duty of obedience to positive law on our duty of self-preservation, comes out strongly in a passage to which we must in a moment refer; but at first Hobbes takes care not to depart too widely from common sense. In several passages he speaks of some of our "natural rights" as inalienable, and in one (to Filmer's disgust) he seems to open a wide door for disobedience, by justifying it in cases where obedience would defeat the end for which our rights are aliened, namely, "the security of a man's person in his life, and in the means of so preserving life as not to be weary of it."[33] But this is exceptional, and on the whole Hobbes' doctrine appears to be that a man ought always to obey the law, but that if he have broken the law, he cannot be expected to submit without resistance to the punishment.[34] In the *Behemoth* he decides that a son ought to kill his own father if commanded by law to do so.[35] But even the *liberty of resisting* punishment is withdrawn in the development of his system. In the religious portions of his political treatises (which

32. *Hobbes' English Works*, vol. III. 119. (This, I think, is introduced for the first time in the *Leviathan*, the parallel passages being II. 17, and IV. 88.)

33. Ibid., III. 120.

34. *Hobbes' English Works*, vol. II. 25, 26.

35. Ibid., VI. 227.

may I think be appealed to, as I see no sufficient reason for believing, with some of his critics, that Hobbes' professions of religion are hypocritical) he decides that a Christian prince, that is, a prince who believes the fundamental article of Christianity, that Jesus is the Christ,[36] is supreme in all matters spiritual, as well as temporal. An infidel prince however is to be obeyed only in temporal matters, not in matters relating to Divine worship. "But what? Must we resist princes when we cannot obey them? Truly, no; for this is contrary to our civil covenant. What must we do then? Go to Christ by martyrdom."[37]

I quote this *firstly* in order to show that Hobbes is not consistent in teaching that we may not disobey law, but may resist punishment, for here the doctrine is exactly reversed, we are to disobey and submit to punishment; *secondly,* because we seem here to have reached a *reductio ad absurdum* of Hobbism. We are not to resist when the infidel prince would make martyrs of us. Why? Because to resist would be "contrary to our civil covenants." But why should we keep our civil covenants? Because we ought to preserve our lives so as not to be weary of them. Thus the desire of self-preservation counsels us to submit to martyrdom. This shews how difficult it is to render the conventional theory conservative.

Hobbes added to the difficulties which lay in his way by maintaining a peculiar psychology, which he has tersely summed up thus, "Now what seems good is pleasant, and relates either to the senses or to the mind. But all the mind's pleasure is glory (or to have a good opinion of one's self), or refers to glory in the end; the rest are sensual or conducing to sensual-

36. Ibid., ii. 306, 307, iii. 590, iv. 179.
37. Ibid., ii. 314–316; iii. 600–602; iv. 186–188.

ity."[38] He greatly exaggerates the force of emulation. Man, according to him, "can relish nothing but what is eminent." He leaves the social desires out of consideration. He did not, as James Mill thinks, mean merely that all our desires *once were* purely self-regarding, but have become social by a process of "mental chemistry" such as Hartley and his school imagined; no, according to Hobbes, our desires always continue to be self-regarding. Thus the whole weight of our duty of keeping our covenants is thrown on reason, that is, the cool settled desire of self-preservation. Man is not naturally a social animal, his joy consists in glory, in comparing himself with other men, and thus he has no social instincts leading him to the civil state, he is only brought to it by a perception that otherwise his life will be "nasty, brutish, short."

I am inclined to think (though there is great risk of such speculations being wrong) that Hobbes was led to exaggerate his account of man's naturally unsocial character by a desire to bring "the state of nature" into discredit. The "state of nature" was the state in which God had created man, it was an ideal state to which civil society should be made to conform. Hobbes thought that there should be no ideal to which political reformers could appeal when preaching disobedience and anarchy. So he pronounced that the state of nature is a state of war. This scandalized Clarendon and other orthodox thinkers, it was calling "nasty" and "brutish" what God had called "very good"; but if we examine the theory calmly it does not seem very objectionable. We have no sooner heard that man is naturally in a state of war than we hear of a faculty called reason, which prompts man to seek peace, and we are told that this faculty

38. Ibid., II. 5.

is just as natural as any other faculty. So the whole theory amounts but to this. If men were irrational, they would quarrel and fight and never form civil states, but *by nature* they are rational, and reason counsels them to seek peace. In fact we have here, as Hume says, only a decomposition of forces. "Human nature being composed of two principal parts, which are requisite in all its actions, the affections and understanding, it is certain that the blind motions of the former, without the direction of the latter, incapacitate men for society; and it may be allowed to consider separately the effects that result from the separate operations of these two component parts of the mind."[39] Hobbes really only performs what Hume thinks "may be allowed." But he lays great stress on the "preposterous conclusions" which, according to Iago, would result "if the balance of our lives had not one scale of reason to poise another of sensuality," and calls the state of men, when deprived of their natural faculty of reason, the "state of nature," because he wishes to discredit one of the "sacramental phrases" of the reforming party, and thus strike a blow at anti-nomianism and anarchy.

Hitherto we have spoken of Hobbes as an apologist for *de facto* governments, and as such he ought to be considered. Though the *Behemoth* is a justification of the Stuarts, he ends it by saying that the sovereignty had passed by a circular motion from Charles I to the Long Parliament, thence to the Rump, thence to Cromwell, thence back again to the Long Parliament, thence to Charles II. So the Rump and Cromwell had really been sovereigns, and the covenants of the nation must, during their rule, have been applicable to them. There appears to me insufficient evidence for saying that Hobbes changed his opinions; he steadily refused to allow of any title to rule save

39. *Treatise*, etc., III. ii. 2.

the title of a *de facto* government. He does not enter at length
into the nice question of when a *de facto* sovereignty ceases, but,
apart from a *de facto*, he knows of no *de jure* sovereign. The
subjects, we learn, cannot get rid of the sovereign by agreement
among themselves, for the sovereign has rights under the social
covenant.[40] In the *de Cive* we learn that the subjects are free if
the land be conquered, if the sovereign abdicate, or if the succession fail.[41] In the *Leviathan* this doctrine is extended, and
the subjects are made free when the king can no longer protect
them.[42] The twentieth law of nature, added in a postscript to
the other nineteen, makes him who protects the subjects sovereign;[43] and this is what Clarendon called "a sly address" to
Cromwell.

It should not however be forgotten that Hobbes does try to
prove that a limited monarchy is an absurdity, a contradiction
in terms, and in the *Behemoth* and the *Dialogue on the Laws*
does try to prove that Charles I was an absolute monarch; and
"an absolute monarch" with Hobbes means a good deal. Such
an one is subject to no laws, and to no positive morality.

Charles was king. The king of England is an absolute monarch: he cannot forfeit one jot of the sovereign power. To attempt to limit his authority was not only a crime, but a sin; it
was the sin of rebellion, which sums up in itself all sins, and
excludes the sinner from salvation. All of this is to be found in
Hobbes' writings; but, says Austin, to call this an apology for
tyranny is "rant."

Hobbes tried to stop the natural course of the conventional

---

40. *English Works* II. 91, 92.
41. Ibid., II. 107.
42. Ibid., III. 208.
43. Ibid., III. 703.

theory, but with ill success; it was too strong for him, and swept on towards modern democracy. We have seen this theory in the works of Hooker, Milton, and Sydney, trying to live at peace with the theory that some men are worthier to rule than others, and that *detur digniori* is the voice of reason. As long as this was the case the conventional theory could never become constructive; it was at best an engine for destroying the claims of hereditary monarchy. We must have some principle which shall decide whose consent it is that we shall require; and this Locke provides. All men, he says, are "creatures of the same species and rank, promiscuously born to all the same advantages of nature, and the use of the same faculties," and therefore they ought to be "equal one amongst another, without subordination or subjection, unless the Lord and Master of them all should by any manifest declaration of His will, set one above another."[44] Of the truth of the assertion that all men are born with the same faculties, and of the legitimacy of the conclusion that therefore there is by nature no subordination or subjection between them, I must again speak. Here let us refer to the way in which Locke obtains his ethical first principles, the principle, for instance, that those to whom God has given equal faculties are by Him intended to be free from all subjection, save that to which they have consented. A short statement of Locke's ethical opinions will not be out of place, as it will shew the way in which the first great apostle of the Rights of Man obtained the premises of his politics.

Things are called good and evil only in reference to pleasure and pain.[45] What is apt to produce pleasure in us we call *good*,

44. *On Govt.* II. 4.
45. *Hum. Under.* II. xx. 2.

for no other reason than because it is apt to produce pleasure.[46] Moral good is the conformity of our voluntary actions to some law whereby good is drawn on us by the will of the law-giver.[47] The only true touchstone of rectitude is the law of God, whereby He directs us to what is best: this law bearing sanctions not only in a future life, but in this life also. This law we discover by the light of nature and by revelation.[48] Apart from revelation, it is reason which discovers this law; in fact, reason *is* the law of nature.[49] The laws of God can be deduced with demonstrative certainty from our idea of a Supreme Being, infinite in power, goodness, and wisdom, on whom we depend, and the idea of ourselves as understanding, rational beings. Our knowledge of the Supreme Being is derived from our intuitive knowledge of our own existence, and our knowledge that there must be some eternal cause of our existence, power, and knowledge.[50] Of the ethical propositions which can be thus deduced with demonstrative certainty, he gives two examples—"Where there is no property there is no injustice," and "No government allows absolute liberty."[51] (Very true, but very useless.) It requires study and reasoning to discover this divine law, but it is easily intelligible and plain to all, for men are furnished with the same faculties.[52] The sum of this is: Men ought to obey the laws of God, deduced by reason from the knowledge we have

46. Ibid., II. xxi. 42.
47. Ibid., II. xxviii. 5.
48. Ibid., II. xxviii. 8–11.
49. *On Govt.* II. 6.
50. *Hum. Under.* IV. x.
51. Ibid., IV. iii. 18.
52. *On Govt.* II. 4, 6, 12.

of God and of ourselves; such obedience being good because it brings us pleasure. But here is a difficulty. Such obedience may be good, but how are we to say that the laws or their Maker are good? Locke calls God good, though he does not, when formally proving the existence of a Supreme Being, prove that goodness is one of His attributes. He should shew that these laws are themselves fitted to secure the pleasure of mankind, or how can he, with his definition of goodness, call them or their Maker good? It is certain, however, that Locke regarded our duties as set us by the laws of God, which can be deduced by reason, and, when laying down a maxim as such a law, he does not make a calculation of consequences, but appeals to the law as discoverable from our knowledge of God. And indeed he held that a man who does not believe in a God cannot know of any moral duties,[53] and thus morality is merged in natural religion.

I believe however that Locke would not have objected to saying that the laws of God direct us to those actions which most conduce to the greatest happiness of the greatest number, and it is probably to this fact that he would have appealed if asked to shew that God is good. But he attempts to transcend utilitarianism by deducing moral laws from our idea of God. In short, his politics are as "meta-political" (to use Coleridge's happy phrase) as those of Kant himself.

What therefore Locke has to do is to deduce the right of every man to be under no government to which he has not consented, from the ideas of God as infinitely wise, good, and powerful, and of ourselves as understanding, rational creatures. He proceeds to shew that men being the workmanship of God, and

---

53. *First Letter on Toleration.*

being His property whose workmanship they are, have no right to destroy themselves or others. They must preserve themselves and not quit their station wilfully, and, when their own preservation comes not into competition, they must preserve the liberty, health, limbs, and goods of others.[54] We have however a right to punish offenders; we may retribute to them what is proportionate to their transgressions, which is so much as may serve for reparation and restraint.[55] But what are the offences which we may punish? Apparently any breaches of the laws of nature, the particulars of which laws it would, Locke thinks, be beside his purpose to enter into.[56] The highest crime of which a man can be guilty is the attempt to get another man into his absolute power, for it may reasonably be concluded that he who would get me into his power without my consent would destroy me if he had a fancy to it.[57] Hence we ought to be free from all absolute power to which we have not given our consent.[58]

Such is the argument by which Locke would deduce the conventional theory from our ideas of God and of ourselves. We are God's property, not our own, therefore we may not destroy ourselves or each other; he who attempts to assume the sovereignty without the consent of the ruled, must be supposed to be intent on destroying them, and therefore commits the greatest of all sins against the law of nature.

Government therefore ought to rest upon the consent of the governed, and the consent of every man is equally valuable. But

54. *On Govt.* II. 6.
55. Ibid., II. 8.
56. Ibid., II. 7–12.
57. Ibid., II. 17–21.
58. Ibid., II. 22.

what are we to consent to? It is of the greatest importance that we should have an exact answer.

Unfortunately, Locke here assumes the place of the historian, and begins to tell us what men *have done;* he allows fictitious history to intrude upon ethics. But we must take the doctrine as we find it. We are told that when any number of men have by the consent of every individual made a community, they have thereby made the community one body with power to act as one body, which is only by the will and determination of the majority. So when once the state is formed, the whole body is to be concluded by the majority. This assertion of the divine right of majorities is most important, and here is the reasoning on which it is based. That which acts any community, being only the consent of the individuals of it, and it being necessary for that which is one body to move one way, it is necessary for that which is one body to move that way whither the great force carries it, which is the consent of the majority: or else it is impossible to act or continue one body, one community, which the consent of every individual united into it agreed that it should, and so every one is bound by that consent to be concluded by the majority.[59] At first this looks like a piece of Social Mechanics, this talk about necessity seems to imply that we are to take a fatalist view of the matter, and say that a body politic *will* always move as the majority of citizens would have it move. Even here the physical analogy breaks down; a body acted on by two unequal opposite forces does not move as if the lesser force did not exist. This however is not what Locke meant, he is not really speaking of what *must* happen, but of what *ought to* happen, and doubtless it is his opinion that men's

59. Ibid., ii. 95, 96.

faculties are equal, which makes him see in the principle that a majority can bind a minority the one possible principle of just government.

But how about after generations? Does the consent of the fathers bind the children to be concluded by the majority? Burke tries to shew that the original contract binds posterity, but Locke resolutely answers that the son is altogether as free as the father. At this point however in Locke's argument, there is a little vacillation. At first we are told that every citizen enters into the covenant when he comes of age. But, it is argued, no government can permit any part of its dominions to be enjoyed by those who do not belong to the community. The original contract is thus supposed "to run with the land," to use a lawyer's phrase. Every person who has possession or enjoyment of any land within the dominions of the government has given his consent to its laws. So far the idea is that, the land being bound by the covenant, every one who has possession or enjoyment of the land gives a tacit consent to the government[60] *"by becoming a member of the society."*[61] But in a few lines all is changed. These tacit covenantors are not members of the society, their obligation begins and ends with the enjoyment of the land,[62] and we are introduced to a fresh set of covenantors who, by actual agreement and express declaration, have given their consent to be of the commonwealth, and are perpetually and indispensably obliged to be and remain unalterably subjects to it: and nothing can make a man a member of the commonwealth but his actually entering into it, by *positive engagement and express promise*

60. Ibid., II. 116–119.
61. Ibid., II. 117.
62. Ibid., II. 120.

and compact.[63] Thus having been told that the son becomes a member of the society by merely enjoying the possessions of his father, we now learn that he is not a member of the community unless he has entered into it by express promise and compact.

I have dwelt at some length on this point because I would shew the exact steps by which the conventional theory leads us to democracy. If men can bind their posterity, then the conventional theory may be perfectly conservative, but then how are we to say that all men are born free? If we are prepared to reject natural freedom we have no need of the conventional theory. If we will not do this, we must say with Locke, that the son is born as free as the father. Then Locke finds a momentary resting-place in the notion of a covenant which binds, not posterity, but the land which posterity occupies. But this will not do, for even if our ethics were bounded by Real Property Law we should admit that not all conditions with which a man may try to burden his successors in title are valid. The moralist would go at least as far as the lawyer in abhorring a perpetuity. Locke tells us that the earth has been given to men in common, and shall one generation be able to deprive its successors of the use of it? So Locke surrenders this doctrine, and seems to think it only necessary as accounting for the way in which *alien residents* become subject to our laws; and then he boldly proclaims that nothing can make any man a subject or member of the commonwealth but his actually entering into it, by positive agreement, and express promise and compact.

One barrier still remains between us and democracy. The majority may institute some legislative body, and surrender certain of the natural rights of the people to this body. It may even

63. Ibid., II. 121.

give the power to one man.[64] After this grant of power the legislator or prince may have certain rights. He holds his power under an agreement, and apparently cannot be cashiered as long as he performs his part of the agreement. I take the following words of Dr. Hutcheson to be a correct account of the proceedings at the Original Convention, as imagined by Locke: "To constitute a state or civil polity in a regular manner these three deeds are necessary—First, a *contract* of each one with all that they should unite into one society to be governed by one counsel; and next, a *decree* or *ordinance* of the people concerning the plan of government, and the nomination of governors; and lastly, another *covenant* or *contract* between these governors and the people, binding the rulers to a faithful administration of their trust and the people to obedience."[65] Here is some little defence against democracy, for by this latter covenant the people are obliged to obedience as long as the rulers do not break their half of the engagement, and it is admitted that the power *may* have been granted to the rulers *for ever.* Even Hobbes is not excluded. He could still say that all rights *have* been surrendered for ever, and that the rulers have on their part made no covenant at all. But Locke is not going to permit the revival of such pretensions. We can learn the conditions of the contract between the rulers and the ruled by considering why it was that men left the state of nature for the social state. It was because they wanted—(1) a known and settled law to decide their controversies; (2) known and indifferent judges; (3) power to enforce the law against criminals.[66] But it is with the intention the better to preserve himself, his life, liberty, and property,

---

64. Ibid., II. 132.
65. *Hutcheson's Introduction to Mor. Phil.* III. 5.
66. *On Govt.* II. 124.

that every man consents to enter the society, and therefore the power of the society ought never to be supposed to extend further than the common good, and is obliged to secure to every man his property (*i.e.*, life, liberty, and estate) by guarding against those defects in the state of nature which induced men to form communities.[67] Hence it follows that the legislative body instituted by the majority of the community—(1) must govern by established laws, (2) must design its laws for no other end ultimately but the good (*i.e.*, pleasure) of the people, (3) must not raise taxes without the consent of the people, for it must not take from any one his property without *"his own consent, i.e., the consent of the majority"*;[68] (4) must not delegate its legislative power.[69] But supposing that there is a dispute between the prince and the people as to whether these conditions have been broken (and surely there well may be such a dispute, for men are not apt to agree as to whether a prince's laws are designed for no other end but the good of the people), who is to decide? "Who shall be judge whether the prince or legislative act contrary to their trust? To this I reply, the people shall be judge."[70]

Thus just when the conventional theory might have been appealed to on the Conservative side, Locke practically abandons it and falls back on Utilitarianism. One of the conditions of their tenure of office is that the rulers shall make laws for no other end ultimately but the good of the people, and if the rulers break this condition, they have no further rights under the

67. Ibid., ii. 123–131.
68. Ibid., ii. 140.
69. Ibid., ii. 134–141.
70. Ibid., ii. 240.

contract. This is to go nearly as far as Hutcheson, who, though he also admits a contract between rulers and ruled, says outright that if greater and more lasting mischiefs are likely to arise from the continuance of a government than from a violent effort to change it, such an effort is both lawful and honourable. Rousseau, we shall see, manages the matter more cleverly, for he admits of no contract between the rulers and the ruled. But at any rate, the barrier between Locke and democracy is a very weak one.

Though Locke comes with a system of rights to liberty and equality deduced from the very idea of God, there runs throughout his politics a tendency to admit that the Utilitarian measure of right and wrong is the true one. "The end of government is the good of mankind."[71] "The public good is the rule and measure of all law-making."[72] And good is pleasure. Locke resembles Hobbes[73] in this respect. He requires his sovereign to be a utilitarian, but holds that we can decide who ought to be sovereign by some surer and readier method than by considering who will make the best laws. Now it is by no means evident that "the end of government" will be attained, or the "measure of all law-making" satisfied, when the governors are appointed by the majority of the people. Thus we may have to say that the only right government (that is, one established by a majority of the people) is not the one best suited to attain the end for which all governments are instituted. Of course, the laws of morality *may* not be harmonious among themselves, but this is a conclusion which we can scarcely come

71. Ibid., II. 229.
72. *First Letter on Toleration.*
73. *On Govt.* III. 322.

to, if we look upon these laws as deduced from the idea of a Being infinite in power, goodness, and wisdom.

Burke has vehemently asserted that the French Liberté was not the Liberty for which our own Whig patriarchs pleaded;[74] but Burke would have found it difficult to show that there was any single article in the Declaration of the Rights of Man for which ample authority could not be found in the writings of the most popular of all English philosophers. It is surprising how little Rousseau added to the essential part of the conventional theory as it was delivered to him by Locke. Of course there is a great external difference between the writings of the cautious, candid Englishman, and those of the brilliant French romance writer, but the difference is external. In Locke we find a constant desire not to "go beyond his brief," while Rousseau will at all hazard turn out a perfectly neat and logical piece of work; but Locke had been obliged to proclaim principles which covered not only his own case, but also the case of Rousseau. The chief improvements which Rousseau introduced into the conventional theory must be shortly noticed.

Locke, we have seen, emphatically asserts that a father cannot alienate the liberty of his children;[75] Rousseau agrees, "un tel don est contraire aux fins de la nature, et passe les droits de la paternité."[76] But Locke holds that the land being bound by the contract, occupation of the land must be taken as evidence of a tacit consent to the government. He however wavers, and

---

74. *Reflections on the Revolution*, etc.

75. *Civ. Govt.* II. 116.

76. [such a surrender is contrary to natural justice, and exceeds the rights of fatherhood.] *Du Contrat Social*, I. iv. [N.B., "Les fins de la nature" means, literally, "the purposes of nature."]

requires an express consent in order that a man may become a subject of the State. Rousseau is at one with him. Unanimity is necessary for the *contrat social*, if any one will not consent he remains outside the State; but, "quand l'État est institué le consentement est dans la résidence; habiter le territoire c'est se soumettre à la souveraineté."[77] This doctrine however would allow that tyranny may become rightful by prescription, so a very characteristic note is added: "Ceci doit toujours s'entendre d'un État libre; car d'ailleurs la famille, les biens, le defaut d'asyle, la necessité, la violence, peuvent retenir un habitant dans le pays malgré lui, et alors son sejour seul ne suppose plus son consentement au contrat, ou à la violation du contrat."[78] This ingenuity is beyond Locke, who, when speaking of residence as a tacit consent, does not make it applicable only to the case of a "free" state; but then he elsewhere does what is almost equivalent, for he will not allow that an usurper—one who obtains power by other ways than those which the laws of the community have prescribed—can have any authority until he has obtained the *actual* consent of the people.[79]

But Rousseau's grand improvement on Locke is that he gets rid of the third of Hutcheson's "three deeds"; he will have no contract between the rulers and the ruled. The first deed, the contract of association, is the only social contract.[80] Here Rous-

77. [once the state is established consent inheres in residence; to inhabit the country is to own its sovereignty.] *Cont. Soc.* v. ii.

78. [This must always be understood to mean a free state; and in addition family matters, property, lack of asylum, necessity, or violence can force someone to stay in a country against his wishes, and then his stay no longer implies in itself his consent to the contract or to its violation.] Ibid., note.

79. *Civ. Govt.* ii. 198.

80. *Cont. Soc.* iv. 16.

seau is at one with Hobbes, who, though for a very different reason, will have no contract between the sovereign and the subjects. Hobbes' account of the proceeding is that the subjects covenant among themselves, the sovereign not being a party.[81] From this we should expect that the sovereign can have no rights under the covenant, and that the covenantors could by mutual agreement annul the contract. But this was not at all what Hobbes wanted, so he imagines, not a contract between rulers and ruled, but a *grant* to the ruler.[82] Rousseau does not admit the contract or the grant; the rulers hold their power not only by, but also during the will of the sovereign people. Now this is a great improvement in the theory: there can be no question as to whether the rulers have kept their part of the engagement. If they be not wanted they may go. After all, however, Locke had gone nearly as far as this, for the rulers may be sent about their business if they make laws for any other end but the good of the people, and Hutcheson had gone quite as far. In fact, with the latter the "third deed" is a mere survival; it is not useful, and must drop off in time.

But Rousseau, in his practical application, does go much further towards democracy than Locke did. "Toute loi," he says, "qui le peuple en personne n'a pas ratifiée est nulle; ce n'est point une loi. Le peuple Anglais pense être libre; il se trompe fort, il ne l'est que durant l'élection des membres du Parlement; si-tôt qu'ils sont élus il est esclave, il n'est rien."[83] How, let us

81. *On Govt.* III. 161.

82. Ibid., II. 91.

83. ["Any law," he says, "which the people have not personally ratified is null; it is not a law. The English people think they are free and in this they are much mistaken. They are free only while members of Parliament are being elected. As soon as this is accomplished they are slaves again; they are nothing."]

ask, would Locke have answered this? He would probably have said that undoubtedly the people of England have a God-given right to make their own laws, but that they do not think it expedient to insist on this right: they cannot, however, lose the right by lapse of time; if they choose to insist on it no one can rightfully object. But though he might make use of an appeal to expediency to stop democracy in practice, he cannot use it to resist the theory that all men have a right which they may enforce if they please, to be under no laws save those to which they have consented. It will be noticed that Locke does not admit that the consent of our representatives is all that we can insist on, for a representative assembly he thinks *may* (though it probably *will* not) infringe the natural rights of the people, *e.g.*, by raising taxes without their consent.[84]

We have seen how Locke gets over the difficulty of identifying the consent of the majority with the consent of the whole; we must have agreed to be concluded by the majority because a body politic must move in one way. And when speaking of taxation he says that a man's property may not be taken without "his own consent, *i.e.*, the consent of the majority."[85] This simple *id est* is too clumsy for Rousseau: he rises to the occasion, and produces a splendid sophism, which I quote at length, because it shows the difficulty of hiding the weak point of the conventional theory:

Mais on demande comment un homme peut être libre, et forcé de se conformer à des volontés qui ne sont pas les siennes. Comment les opposans sont-ils libres et soumis à des loix auxquelles ils n'ont pas consenti? Je réponds que la question est mal

---

84. *Civ. Govt.* II. 138.
85. Ibid., II. 140.

posée. Le citoyen consent a toutes les loix, même a celles qu'on passe malgré lui, et même a celles qui le punissent quand il ose en violer quelqu'une. La volonté constante de tous les membres de l'État est la volonté générale; c'est par elle qu'ils sont citoyens et libres. Quand on propose une loi dans l'assemblée du peuple, ce qu'on leur demande n'est pas précisément s'ils approuvent la proposition ou s'ils la rejettent; mais si elle est conforme ou non à la volonté générale qui est la leur; chacun en donnant son suffrage, dit son avis la-dessus, et du calcul des voix se tire la déclaration de la volonté générale. Quand donc l'avis contraire au mien l'emporte, cela ne preuve autre chose sinon que je m'é-tois trompé et que ce que j'estimois être la volonté générale, ne l'étoit pas. *Si mon avis particulier l'eut emporté, j'aurois fait autre chose que ce que j'avois voulu, c'est alors que je n'aurois pas été libre.*[86]

Now when Sydney says that civil liberty is an exemption from all laws to which we have not consented, this sounds plausible. Liberty is absence of restraint imposed upon us by other men, and it is plausible to say that we cannot require a liberty

86. [But one may ask how a man can be free and yet forced to obey wills other than his own. How can an opposition be free and yet subject to laws it did not consent to? I would reply that the question is wrongly put. The citizen consents to all the laws, even those enacted against his wishes, even those which punish him when he dares to break one of them. The enduring will of all the members of the polity is the general will. This is what makes them citizens and free people. When a law is proposed, the people being assembled, what they are asked is not precisely whether they approve or reject the proposition, but whether it is consistent or not with their general will. Each one, in giving his vote, expresses his opinion on the issue and from the reckoning of their overall views is drawn the general will. So when an opinion contrary to mine embodies it, this proves only that I was wrong and that what I thought was the general will was not. *If my particular opinion had prevailed, I would have done something other than what I wished. This is when I would not have been free.*] *Cont. Soc.* v. ii.

from self-imposed restraint. But when Rousseau tells us that a man is not free, though he be under no restraints whatsoever, unless the majority of the people wish that he should be under no restraint, we seem to have wandered far out of the right road. The question must force itself upon us, Have we not been pursuing an object which constantly retires before us? We say that men should be under no laws save those to which they have given their consent; we say that Hobbes' fictitious consent will not do. Consent must be real—it must be the consent of all, and, trying to make the consent real and universal, we land ourselves in democracy; and yet we find that an individual may still be under many restraints to which only an ingenious sophistry can say that he has consented. If what we want be freedom from all restraint not strictly self-imposed, democracy cannot be the ultimate ideal of the conventional theory.

Even in Rousseau we already see rising an opinion that democracy does not give us any security for that liberty which is valuable, or else what is the meaning of his eulogy on the state of nature, the state in which there were no laws? But the world could only be convinced that democracy is not necessarily a security for that liberty which men desire, by a great practical experiment.

We must now return to England, and we notice that during the quiet time which succeeded our Revolution the conventional theory is put away, and even falls into discredit. One of the first blows struck at the Original Contract came from Locke's pupil Shaftesbury, who, looking at the interests of mankind as harmonious, and constantly dwelling on our social instincts, thought that civil societies might well arise and continue without any contract. Ascribing the perception of moral differences to a sense, or taste, rather than to reason, he opposes

that tendency of "rational" moralists to resolve all our duties
into truthfulness or fidelity, which tendency had added force to
the conventional theory. "The natural knave," he says, "has the
same reason to be a civil one, and may dispense with his politic
capacity as oft as he sees occasion. 'Tis only his word stands in
his way. A man is obliged to keep his word. Why? Because he
has given his word to keep it. Is not this a notable account of
the original of moral justice and the rise of civil government
and allegiance!"[87] Again, Shaftesbury was brought by another
road to resist the principles of Locke, for Locke derived our
political rights from the idea of God, and this founding of morality on religion Shaftesbury condemned with unusual asper-
ity, it throws "all order and virtue out of the world."[88] His
aesthetic ethics were much less likely to lead to inalienable, indefeasible rights than the jural, religious, semi-Puritan ethics
of his master.

But in no book is the reaction against the politics which give
Divine rights to kings or to majorities more marked than in the
Essay on Man. That reaction must have been at its height when
Pope wrote—

> For forms of government let fools contest:
> Whate'er is best administer'd is best.

It is the prevailing optimism of the time, the optimism so well
illustrated by Shaftesbury and Pope, which led to this contempt
of political speculation. Good government appears to these op-
timists a matter of no great difficulty. After all, governments
can do but little towards making men happy or unhappy. Virtue, thinks Pope, alone gives the best happiness; external goods,

87. *Freedom of Wit and Humour,* Pt. 3, Sec. 1.
88. *Letter to a Student,* VII.

the only goods which governments can provide, are comparatively worthless. This optimism I believe to be a great exaggeration.

That true self-love and social are the same,

requires more proof than has yet been given of it, and Shaftesbury's attempt to find such a proof is to this day one of the best as well as the most ingenious. But it was high time that the social part of our nature should be brought into prominence, and that we should be shewn to have other motives leading us to civil intercourse, besides our sense of a duty owed to God, and our fear of God, and our fellow-men.

The harmony of the time was broken by Mandeville's assertion that civil society is far from an unmixed good, that crafty politicians have for their own purposes induced men to subject themselves to laws. Thus Mandeville assisted Rousseau in setting up a state in which there is no civil government as an ideal. Men, said Rousseau and Mandeville, have been coerced, or cozened into submitting to law, and the question arises as to whether civil society is not a mistake. It was this line of thought which did much towards proving that the ultimate ideal of those who would free men from all restraints not strictly self-imposed is not to be found in democracy. Burke makes use of arguments with which Mandeville had familiarized the world when he insists against Bolingbroke that all that can be said for natural as against revealed religion, can equally well be said for natural as against civil society. "Shew me an absurdity in religion, and I will undertake to shew you a hundred for one in political laws and institutions."[89] Now, so well did Burke put the arguments against civil society, that there were some who

89. Burke, *Vindication of Natural Society.*

thought that he spent his whole life in vainly attempting to answer them. Such an one was Godwin, the author of the *Political Justice,* a book, now chiefly known as the exciting cause of *Malthus on Population,* but one of the best productions of English democracy. Godwin *expressly* accepts Burke's *reductio ad absurdum* of Bolingbroke as a really sound argument.[90] This, coupled with the doctrine of the perfectibility of man, due to the fact that his voluntary actions spring from opinion and that he is rapidly attaining true opinion, led Godwin to look upon democracy as merely a stage on the road to liberty—a road which will end in the complete abolition of government. I have said this in order to shew how the teaching of Mandeville and Rousseau, that men made an error in letting themselves be deprived of their natural liberty, affected that stream of thought which, starting from our commonwealthsmen and Locke, at first takes its course towards democracy.

Before we speak of Hume, who fitly closes that period of our Political Philosophy which lies between the two revolutions, we must refer shortly to the course of ethical speculation in England. During the time of civil strife our political philosophers were too eager to find some answer to the question, "Who ought to rule?" They tried to supply the place of an answer to the more fundamental question, "What ought a ruler to do?" by some piece of fictitious history, a direct grant from God to some man and his heirs, or an original contract. But we can scarcely hope to answer this latter question until we have settled what is to be the supreme principle of ethics. For if there be some one supreme principle according to which all men ought always to act (and our philosophers, Bentham no less than those whom he ridicules, always assume that this is the case),

90. *Political Justice,* B. 1.

then the answer to the fundamental question of ethics, what ought men to do, must be, or include an answer to the fundamental question of politics, how ought men to act in their civil relations. "Le but de l'association, quelque nombreuse qu'elle soit, ne peut être essentiellement autre que le but de chacun des êtres associés; et la loi suprême de l'individu sera la loi suprême de l'état."[91] Hence, for the progress of political philosophy, it was necessary that the various possible answers to the question of ethics should be unravelled and distinguished. Whether we get any nearer to a settlement of this question may be doubted, but it is certainly more possible to understand what the exact issue is in these days than it was when Hobbes opened the controversy. Hobbes found the orthodox unprepared. He startled the world by his proclamation of "glory" and "sensuality" as our only motives, and of the will of the sovereign as the only standard of right, and his opponents caught up the first weapons which came to their hand without being nice in their choice. It was retorted that there is a difference between right and wrong, independent of all positive law, a difference pointed to by Revealed and Natural Religion, Reason, Conscience, the interest of mankind, and even enlightened Selfishness, and an indiscriminate use was made of these as a defence for morality, and civil liberty. Political writers like Clarendon found no difficulty in withstanding Hobbes by appealing to numerous principles, which the moralist sees are not necessarily compatible with each other.

In the first place it became necessary to exclude revealed reli-

91. [The purpose of the association, however numerous it may be, cannot be essentially different from the purpose of each one of the persons associated; and the supreme law of the individual will be the supreme law of the state.] Saint-Hilaire, *Politique d'Aristote,* p. xi.

gion from the coalition. Both Cumberland and Clarke keep religious considerations out of sight when setting up their criteria of right action; for the truth of religion can scarcely be proved without the help of some independent standard of right. Again, the difficulty of calling God good—if His will be the measure of goodness—made the establishment of a moral system based on natural religion seem to most men illegitimate; Locke is here an exception. But a further disruption was necessary. Clarke held that "the good of the universal creation does always coincide with the necessary truth and reason of things," and that, were we in possession of an infinite understanding, all morality might be founded on "considerations of public utility."[92] But Butler on the one hand, and Hume on the other, made a lasting breach between the morality of conscience and the morality of general utility.

To Hume fairly belongs the credit, or blame, of being the founder of modern Utilitarianism. It is true that the opposition to Utilitarianism was roused, not so much by his writings as by those of Paley and Bentham. This was likely to be the case, for Hume approached ethics much more in the spirit of Aristotle than in that of a moral preacher. Morality was an existing fact, to be explained if possible. He scarcely draws any distinction between *what ought to be* and *what men think ought to be;* for, as he says, with regard to morals, general opinion is the only standard by which controversy can be decided.[93] It was because he took this view of the matter that his attack on the conventional theory did not produce so great an effect as the attacks of Paley and Bentham. Still there can be no doubt that both Paley and

92. *Evidences,* p. 223.
93. *Essays,* ii. xii.

Bentham owed their conception of morality to Hume. And when they make their attempts to shew that the ordinary rules of morality really aim at utility, they can only follow Hume, and follow him at a considerable distance. The Benthamites have been rather ungrateful to Hume, apparently because he differed from them on the purely psychological question of the origin of the moral sense,[94] but the fact remains that all that can be called a "proof" of Utilitarianism is due to the suggestions of Hume, and that in this line of argument he has never been surpassed.

Directly Utilitarianism has fairly separated itself from other moral systems it begins its attack on the original contract. Hutcheson can scarcely be called an Utilitarian in ethics, but when he comes to politics he becomes distinctly Utilitarian. "The end of all civil power is acknowledged by all to be the safety and happiness of the whole body; any power not naturally conducive to that end is unjust."[95] He still maintains that there ought to be an original contract with its "three deeds," but this has become a mere fiction. When we turn to Hume's works we can see the gradual process by which he freed himself from the conventional theory. We have two editions of his ethical opinions. A change, if not in his views, at least in his language, is discoverable as we pass from the one to the other. In the *Treatise on Human Nature,* though he expressly states that our political duties do not and cannot depend on promises, he uses words only fitted to express the old theory of the original contract. Thus, when considering the duty of justice, he speaks

94. *E.g.,* James Mill, *Fragment on Mackintosh* (ed. 1870), p. 264. J. S. Mill, *Dissert. and Discuss.* (2nd ed.), vol. ii. p. 455.

95. *Introduction to Moral Philosophy.*

of "a convention entered into by all the members of the society to bestow stability on the possession of external goods," &c.— the old phrases lingering on after their meaning has vanished.[96] But these expressions are not to be found in the *Inquiry concerning the Principles of Morals.* He had published an essay on the original contract,[97] which puts forward the arguments afterwards used by Paley[98] and Bentham[99] in their most telling form. Hume had not yet made the acquaintance of Rousseau, he only knew of the conventional theory as a piece of Whiggism, for since Locke's time the theory had been asleep in England. But the argument is equally fitted to meet the democratic doctrine, and the conservative imitation of it. From Hume's day we may date the rise of a definite philosophical antagonism to the conventional theory. Such an antagonism had never before existed, for since Filmer and Mackenzie (who can scarcely be called philosophers) had been conquered by Locke and Sydney, the only choice for the politician had been between different forms of the conventional theory. Doubtless there had been many men who had seen through the pretensions of this theory (Shaftesbury had), but they had not provided a substitute, and Utilitarianism is a substitute.

One more word as to Hume. He proclaimed that politics might be made a science.[100] This was no new assertion, for Hobbes and Locke had gone this length. But Hobbes and Locke thought that geometry should be the model for politics.

---

96. *Treatise,* etc., III. ii.
97. *Essays,* II. xii.
98. *Mor. and Pol. Phil.,* VI. iii.
99. *Fragment on Govt.,* I. xxxvi., *and note.*
100. *Essays,* I. iii.

Neither the one nor the other had shewn the least appreciation of the use of history. Like their contemporaries, they looked upon history not as an account of certain general streams of tendency, but as a collection of anecdotes from which apt illustrations of *à priori* theories might now and then be gleaned. We might describe Hobbes' method, in Mill's language, as the deduction of ethology from psychology, without a verification from history. The seventeenth century revolt against Aristotle is often looked upon as the revolt of induction against deduction. But however true this may be of metaphysics it is wholly untrue of politics. The deductive mind of Hobbes revolted against the cautious induction of Aristotle. Hallam[101] notwithstanding, there is no philosopher who has shewn so little appreciation of the inductive method as Hobbes.[102] In Hume we see the first beginnings (if we except the remarkable work of Harrington) of a scientific use of history. Psychology and history provide evidence for a science of politics. We cannot afford to neglect either; we cannot afford to neglect history with Hobbes, or to plead for the pure Baconian method with Macaulay.[103] Hume, in his short Essays on Politics, tries to use both kinds of evidence, and, though without any parade of system, follows that method which John Mill has described as the proper one for social and political investigations.

To return. At last there appears that outcome of the conventional theory, the *Declaration of the Rights of Man*. It has often been said that there should have been a Declaration of the Duties of Man as well. The reply that the one implies the other is

101. *Hist. Lit.*, vol. III. ch. iii.
102. Hobbes describes his own method, *On Govt.*, III. xi–xii.
103. *Utilitarian Theory of Government.*

obvious, but unsatisfactory. There are many good reasons why a political philosopher should concern himself with duties and not with rights.

(1) It is certain that the rights of Man are not legal rights. They must be what are called moral rights. But supposing that we can attach any definite meaning to the phrase "moral rights," nothing that we can do will ever deprive the word "rights" of its legal savour. We have seen how the expression "laws of nature" may lead to anarchy, but the word "rights" is far more *positive* than even the word "laws."

(2) But if we rigorously exclude the idea of positive legal rights, we have still a whole bundle of ambiguities. An example will shew this. We say that *A* has a moral right to receive £5 from *B*. We may mean simply that it is *B*'s duty to pay that sum. Or that if *A* chooses to force *B* to pay, no one ought to prevent him. Or that other people ought to force *B* to pay, and this they ought to do either by the force of law, or by the force of public opinion. Let me for a moment invent a term or two. If we merely mean that *B* ought to pay, then *A* has a *moral claim*. If we mean that if *A* forces *B* to pay, no one ought to interfere, or that other people ought to force *B* to pay by the sanction of popular opinion, then *A* has *a moral right*. If we mean that third parties ought to oblige *B* to pay by making some law to that effect, then *A* has an *ideal legal right*. This analysis is not complete but must suffice.

(3) Our moral claims and moral rights depend in some measure on positive law. We say that *A* has a moral right to £5 from *B*. We may mean that *B* ought to pay, and public opinion ought to make him pay, *the law of the land being what it is;* or that *B* ought to pay, and public opinion ought to make him pay, *whatever may be the law of the land.*

For all these reasons "rights" should be left to their proper owners, the lawyers. If the rights of man mean anything definite, they can be translated into terms of duty, and it is very advisable that this should be done. Let us take an actual case. Locke and Rousseau would agree in saying that men have a right to be equal. Now this may mean that no one ought to do anything tending to inequality; or that public opinion ought to prevent anyone from doing anything tending to inequality; or that a law ought to be made to punish those who do anything tending to inequality. Again, it may mean that the first, or the first and second of these propositions are true, *law being what it is,* or are true *whatever law may be.*

This is extremely brief and incomplete, the ambiguities of "moral rights" are not exhausted, they are scarcely exhaustible; but enough has been said to shew that we should look on a philosophy of rights with suspicion.

We must now consider what were the philosophic weapons which Englishmen had to oppose to the Rights of Man. It would be unfair to say that Burke used any one weapon, for he used all, and Coleridge is right in saying that he was not very consistent in his use of them. He could be a maintainer of inalienable rights against the calculators, a reckoner of expediency against the preachers of inalienable rights. But Burke has, and has justly, the reputation of being a great philosophic statesman; he shews a desire to get to first principles, and this is the desire of the philosopher. So we may fairly dissect his theories as if they were but the theories of a system-maker.

Now, throughout his works on the Revolution, the two most successful lines of argument are the religious and the utilitarian. He could easily shew that the revolution was opposed to Christianity. He could shew that a great deal of unhappiness resulted from the subversion of the old social order. But he tried to do more than this. Like Hobbes he tried to wrest the conventional theory out of his adversaries' hands. In his *Reflections on the Revolution,* he takes pains to prove, as against Dr. Price, that the rights of choosing our governors, and of cashiering them for misconduct, were not claimed by this nation in 1688. Again, in the Appeal to the old Whigs, he would shew that the party to which he still professed to belong was not committed to the principles of 1789. To a certain extent he was successful. He could shew that Somers in drawing the Bill of Rights was careful to base the English Revolution on necessity. He could say that he did not wish to be a better Whig than Somers, who held that the revolt against James could only be justified by a *privilegium,* and *privilegium non transit in exemplum.* He could shew that the managers of Sacheverell's trial had been at pains to accuse the Doctor on special, not on general grounds; it was not Revolution, but the Revolution of 1688 which was justifiable. But then this proves little. Somers had to scrape together a majority, he wanted (as Macaulay says) not to frame a valid syllogism, but to secure 200 votes by his major and 200 more by his conclusion.[104] That James had broken the original contract, that he had abdicated, that he had left the country, were all put forward as reasons for calling in William. Besides, as Mackintosh shews,[105] Somers and Maynard, when pressed by the Tory Lords, admitted that William was an elected king. Nor was it likely that Walpole and Jekyl would argue for sweeping principles when all they wanted was a conviction. More than this is required if Burke would convince us of the thorough

104. *Hist. Engl.*
105. *Vindiciae Gallicae.*

novelty of the French doctrines. We may not wish to be better Whig statesmen than Somers, we cannot hope to be more truly Whig philosophers than Somers' friend Locke. Coleridge was far more right than Burke, he knew that the French doctrines of liberty and equality were of no sudden growth. Even Coleridge does not trace these doctrines to their source. Coleridge's friend Sydney had gone nearly as far as Coleridge's enemy Locke. Locke did not invent many new political doctrines, his materials were ready to hand; he did but define them more sharply, systematize them more accurately, and reject all that was inconsistent with them. Burke is really much hampered by this notion that he is attacking principles of mushroom growth, the fancies of a few atheistic "garreteers"; this prevents his striking at the real root of the doctrines he hated. He will not break loose from the original contract. Like Hobbes, he will try to shew that we have surrendered some parts of our natural liberty once for all. Only he will find a historic support for this theory. The original contract was confirmed at the Revolution, and was reconfirmed by the Acts of Settlement. And here is a real fact to rest upon, Parliament did profess to bind themselves their heirs and posterities for ever, therefore we are for ever bound.[106]

Hume had answered this argument some thirty years in advance: "Let not the establishment of the Revolution deceive us. . . . It was only the majority of seven hundred who determined that change for near ten millions. I doubt not, indeed, but the bulk of these ten millions acquiesced willingly in the determination, but was the matter left in the least to their choice?"[107] Burke, of course, would reply that the majority of

106. *Reflections*, etc.
107. *Essays*, II. xii.

seven hundred was constitutionally competent to bind the rest. But how came this about? Why were they constitutionally competent to do this? The only answer that the conventional theory can supply is, that they were so under the terms of some older compact. So at last we get back to the *original* contract, for obviously no subsequent ratification which is only binding because made under the terms of that contract can add any force to our original obligation.

So Burke must hold that previous to any social contract the father can bind the son, or else the original contract and all proceedings founded thereon are not obligatory on us. Burke said that he was a Whig; but here he is at issue with the great apostle of Whiggism, who states with emphasis that the father cannot bind the son. Now Hobbes, in trying to make the conventional theory Conservative artfully slurs over this point, managing to speak as if the covenant had been made once for all, and at the same time as if it was made by each successive generation. But Burke distinctly holds that the father can bind the son, thinking however that this is the result of the original contract, which, as I say, it cannot be. The power of binding posterity must be independent of the contract, or else the contract itself has no force.

We must now face this difficulty: "Can a father bind his posterity by his contracts?" Burke and Dr. Whewell say "Yes," Locke and the Utilitarians say "No." Let us see what popular opinion says. That a father can bind his children to the full extent of what they receive from him by bequest or inheritance is a principle of law which has generally, though not always, the support of positive morality. But that a father can bind his children beyond this extent could never be made law. *A* covenants to build a school, and, his children being otherwise provided for, bequeaths all his property to a hospital, leaving his covenant unfulfilled. Popular opinion would sanction a law obliging the hospital trustees to build the school, but it would certainly not sanction a law obliging the children to build the school, nor would it consider it *morally* obligatory on them to do so, even if the hospital trustees evaded their obligation. Common morality does not require the son to keep his father's covenants *quâ* son, but *quâ* heir, devisee, or legatee. And it will be noticed that in Dr. Whewell's argument against Paley the cases of hereditary obligation chosen are cases in which the ancestor's property has passed to his descendants. So if popular opinion allow the force of these lasting covenants, it is only when they "run with" the possession of property. This is the straw at which Locke catches, just before he makes up his mind to require an *express* consent from every citizen. But what says the English law? Any number of lives in being twenty-one years and a few months, that is the limit to your power over real property. But it may be said that this is the outcome of the contract, and is not prior thereto. But will popular morality go further than the English law? Certainly not at present; if the length of time for which settlements are valid is altered, it will not be lengthened. For centuries the law has abhorred a perpetuity. And why? Because it is "contrary to public policy." Are we then to believe that it is not contrary to public policy that we should be bound by a contract made by our ancestors when they first left that state of nature which they probably were never in? I must repeat that any subsequent proceeding of those who, under the original contract had power to settle the government of this country, cannot be binding on us, unless the contract under which they held the power could be binding on us.

Paine perhaps exaggerates when he says, "There never did, there never will, and there never can exist a Parliament, or any description of men, or any generation of men, in any country, possessed of the right or the power of binding posterity 'to the end of time.' . . . and therefore all such clauses, acts, or declarations by which the makers attempt to do what they have neither the right nor the power to do, nor the power to execute, are themselves null and void."[108] We should probably add these words—"if they do not conduce to the good, the happiness, or the morality of the nation." Such clauses are rather "voidable" than "void." But Paine is far nearer common sense than Burke is; those "primary morals," "untaught feelings unvitiated by pedantry," to which Burke appeals are quite against him. No man really conceives that his duty to obey the Queen or the laws depends even in the least degree on the fact that some ancestor of his may possibly have promised that he should do so.

But Burke himself was not satisfied with this, and falls back into a sort of scepticism. To this he had always been prone. In his first work we see its germ in a distrust of human reason, which can easily "make the wisdom and power of God in his creation appear to many no better than foolishness."[109] This germ developes, until we find him railing against philosophy, appealing to "prejudices cherished all the more because they are prejudices," describing the heart of the metaphysician as pure, unmixed, defecated, dephlegmated evil.[110] But this strain of language, this assertion that in morals and politics, reason should yield to prejudice, is not natural to Burke. When he de-

108. *Rights of Man.*
109. *Vindication,* etc.
110. *Letter to a Noble Lord.*

scribes his own reforms, we do not hear that they were dictated by untaught feeling. No, "I have," he says, "ever abhorred . . . all the operations of opinion, fancy, inclination, and will in the affairs of government, where only a sovereign reason, paramount to all forms of legislation, should dictate."[111] The passage from which this is quoted was written near the close of his life, it shews Burke still proud of having been a philosophic reformer, still proud that great and learned economists (probably including Adam Smith) had communicated to him upon some points of "their immortal works," works not dictated by "cherished prejudices."

But Burke was like Reid, he thought that he could play the plain man among philosophers, and the philosopher among plain men. Why, we must ask, did Burke in arguing against the friends of the Jacobins descend from principles to prejudices? Burke has defended himself against the charge of quitting his party, but we do not need this apology to shew us how thorough a Whig he was to the last. No perception of the badness of its results could bring him to abandon the conventional theory. His scepticism is the result; he will neither give up the old doctrine, that all rightful government must rest on the consent of the ruled, nor accept the only legitimate deduction from this principle. So hiding his meaning in a cloud of words, he in effect repeats over and over again that the doctrine of the rights of man is true in theory but false in practice. Here is a specimen of his philosophy. "The pretended rights of these theorists are all extremes; and in proportion as they are metaphysically true, they are morally and politically false. The rights of men are in a sort of middle, incapable of definition, but not impossible to

111. Ibid.

be discerned. . . . Political reason is a computing principle, adding, subtracting, multiplying, and dividing morally and not metaphysically or mathematically true moral denominations."[112] Some examples of principles metaphysically true, but morally and politically false, of moral as opposed to mathematical and metaphysical addition, would not have been thrown away. But what this and many other similar passages really mean is, that Burke will not surrender the premises but will reject the conclusion.

If Burke could but have brought himself to deny that these "metaphysic rights" have any existence, he would have struck the French philosophy the heaviest blow it ever received. But for a really convincing argument against the conventional theory we must turn from Burke to Bentham. Bentham's *Anarchical Fallacies*[113] is one of his best works. It was written before he, perhaps influenced by James Mill, took that peculiar view of human nature which made him think democracy the only form of government tolerable by the Utilitarian. Bentham hated the claim of "metaphysic rights" no less than Burke did, and bolder than Burke, he denied their existence. He insists on having every word in the French declaration explained. What is a right? Are you using "can," "is," and "ought to be" as synonyms? Such and such like questions he showers down, questions which Sieyes would have found it difficult to answer. The Third Article of the Declaration was a statement of the conventional theory. "The principle of every sovereignty resides essentially in the nation. No body of men, no single individual can exercise authority which does not expressly issue from

112. *Reflections*, etc.
113. *Bentham's Works*, II. 491.

thence." If this had been presented as a naked proposition, I believe that Locke, Sydney, Milton, and even Hooker would have accepted it. Bentham replies—The first sentence is perfectly true, perfectly harmless, where there is no obedience there is no government. When we come to the second clause, we meet "the ambiguous and envenomed *'can'*." *Can* not rulers exercise more power than has been expressly committed to them by the nation? They do. This is not the meaning. It must mean that all laws hitherto made are void. What are you going to do to prevent laws being void? The whole nation must consent—women, children, all. If women and children are not part of the nation, what are they? Cattle? "Indeed, how can a single soul be excluded when all men, all human creatures, are, and are to be equal in regard to rights, in regard to all such rights, without exception or reserve." There is much more of such argument, obvious perhaps, but tending to shew how unsatisfactory a support the rights of man afford for human happiness. The whole argument might be summed up in the question— If the assertion of these rights of man does not lead to human happiness, are you right in asserting them? If it is not right to assert them, in what sense can they be called rights?

Of course, it is in many ways absurd to compare Bentham with Burke, but Bentham supplies just the one thing which always seems wanting in Burke's denunciations of Jacobinism. Burke always feared lest in rooting up revolutionary principles he would root up the principles for which he and his forerunners had contended.

It may be added that this exposure of Anarchical Fallacies was intended as a pendent to the Book of Fallacies, for if the two be read together it will be seen that there is little justice in either of the contradictory accusations that have lately been made against Bentham; (1) that he made law the measure of justice, (2) that in advocating law reforms of secondary importance he sacrificed what was of primary importance—respect for law.

The doctrine of the rights of man returned from France to England with all the latest improvements. We must once more refer to the argument on which it is based. Locke says in effect that God has made all men equal, and that this must be taken as evidence of God's intention that there should be no subordination among them save such as results from consent. Now there is much plausibility in this argument, and it was open to Locke and to Rousseau. But it was scarcely one which some of their followers could use, for the best of reasons, namely, that they did not believe that God had made man at all. Tom Paine could only use it by substituting "nature" for "God," and when this is done the argument ceases to be plausible. If we cease to believe that the original equality of man was produced by a Being infinite in goodness and wisdom, there seems to be no reason for treating men as equals when they have become unequals.

The defence of the doctrine in Mackintosh's answer to Burke is interesting, because it is a piece of philosophy in the transitional style; it wavers between Locke and Hume. Mackintosh argues[114] that Burke admits the existence of natural equal rights in all men. Some of these we surrender, but as each surrenders an equal portion, the remaining portions of all must be equal. All men have an equal right to share in the government. But then he turns round—he must have read Hume, and may have read Bentham's *Fragment*. He would leave out "prope" in the line, "Ipsa utilitas justi prope mater et aequi." "Justice is expe-

114. *Vindiciae Gallicae.*

diency," but he adds, "it is expediency speaking by general maxims into which reason has consecrated the experience of mankind. Every general principle of justice is demonstrably expedient, and it is utility alone that confers on us a moral obligation." But though these rights arise from expediency, "the moment the moral edifice is reared its basis is hid from the eye for ever." . . . "It then becomes the perfection of virtue to consider not whether an action be useful, but whether it be right." He then proceeds to argue in the familiar way that the expedience philosophy does not require us to always calculate the expedience of an action, such calculation being itself inexpedient.

But this will not do. The rule forbidding calculation is not a rule for the philosopher laying down his middle axioms; it is a rule for the practical man who has to act in a hurry, and will very likely count himself for more than one. The principle of equality is a principle of justice. "Every principle of justice is demonstrably expedient." Then why not demonstrate the expedience of equality? Because that men should be equal is a maxim into which reason has consecrated the experience of mankind? Surely not. We cannot, at all events, take so important a principle upon trust as being that basis of the moral edifice which is hidden from the eye for ever. If Utilitarianism be once allowed to be at the base of the rights of man, Burke's reply would be crushing. Mackintosh, it may be noticed, afterwards surrendered both Utilitarianism and democracy.

But while the conventional theory was falling into discredit among English philosophers it was proclaimed as a necessary truth by no less a person than Kant. The key-stone of his jurisprudence is the idea of freedom. Law ought to minimize the external restraints to free action.[115] We however meet with an-

115. *Rechtslehre.*

other notion of freedom, and this a familiar one. "Freiheit . . . ist die Befugniss, keinen aüsseren Gesetzen zu gehorchen, als zu denen ich meine Beistimmung habe geben können."[116] Kant was a republican. The republican constitution is, he thinks, "die einzige, welche aus der Idee des ursprünglichen Vertrags hervorgeht auf der alle rechtliche Gesetzgebung eines Volks gegründet sein muss."[117] But by republicanism he does not mean democracy. "Der Republicanismus ist das Staatsprincip der Absonderung der ausführenden Gewalt (der Regierung) von der gesetzgebenden."[118]

What exactly Kant meant by saying that all right laws must be grounded on the idea of an Original Contract, and that we are free when under no laws to which we could not have given our consent, must here be left undetermined. But doubtless it was in imitation of Kant that Coleridge refused to give up the conventional theory. Coleridge has elaborately exposed that "metapolitical" system which attempts to evolve an idea of government out of the pure reason. His attack is directed against Rousseau, but is still more applicable to Kant. He himself is in politics a Utilitarian, a zealous advocate for deriving the various forms and modes of government from human prudence, and of deeming that just which experience has found to be expedient.[119] This being so he does what we should expect, he throws

116. [Freedom . . . is the right to obey no other laws except those to which I have been able to give my consent.] *Entwurf zum ewigen Frieden.*

117. [the only one arising from the idea of the original contract, on which all correct legislation of a people must be grounded.]

118. [Republicanism is the constitutional principle of separation of the executive power (of the government) from the legislative.]

119. *The Friend,* Essay III.

over the original contract. But he cannot give up the last fragment of the conventional theory. He introduces an "ever-originating contract" between the subjects and the sovereign. "If there be any difference between a government and a band of robbers, an act of consent must be supposed on the part of the people governed."[120] Supposed! What would Coleridge have said if he had caught Paley affirming that the difference between right and wrong depends upon a supposition? If we are not going—and Coleridge most certainly was not—to require an actual consent, why ever should we require a supposed consent? Coleridge's sole support for this teaching is an argument addressed to Paley, namely, that whatever Hume might do, a clergyman ought to know that God has authorized the conventional theory by his own example: the relation of mankind as a body spiritual to the Saviour at its head is styled a covenant. But this is trifling. Christians believe that God has actually made promises to them, and that they have actually made promises to God. Are we to say that these promises are "supposed"?

Lastly, Dr. Whewell espoused the cause of an "ever-originating" contract. He thinks "the social compact ... expresses in one phrase the mutual relations of the governors and governed, and of all classes one with another; the reciprocal character of their rights; the possibility of the obligations of one party ceasing, in consequence of some act done by another party; the duty of fidelity and respect to the Constitution; and the condemnation of those who violate or disregard such duties."[121] This is true, but the expression "social compact" im-

120. Ibid., Essay II.
121. *Elements*, § 849.

plies much more than this, it implies that the duties of the governors and the governed depend upon the existence of some agreement; it implies that had there not been some social agreement, men's duties would not have been what they now are. The social compact is quite unnecessary to Dr. Whewell's system, for he admits a special duty of Order; and this, not the duty of keeping promises, is the origin of our duty to respect the Constitution. And indeed he expressly says that "Government has rights which no contract among the subjects could give."[122] This being so, the consent of the subjects not being required in order to make a government rightful, it is surely a mistake to use an expression which was intended to imply, and does still imply, that men have "a right" to be under no government save one which exists by consent. It is also advisable that anti-Utilitarian moralists should cease to use a phrase which points to a defect in the systems of their predecessors, of which their own systems are not guilty. Hitherto the attacks on the conventional theory have come from professed Utilitarians, while their opponents have only surrendered the doctrine which bases the duty of obedience to civil law on the duty of keeping promises, with great reluctance. It would certainly be well that the anti-Utilitarians should clear themselves from the charge of not being able to give any account of our political duties, without falling back upon a principle which either lands us in democracy or has to be turned aside from its natural course by some fiction. It was not unnatural, we repeat, that the conventional theory should have found advocates among moralists who yet were no friends to democracy; for (1) many moralists have been accustomed to see in the duty of keeping

122. Ibid., § 828.

promises the duty most directly and obviously dictated by reason, and (2) those who take the jural view of morality, and include all duties in the general duty of obeying law (*i.e.*, divine
or natural law), may easily omit to find a place for the special
duty of obeying the law of the land. But Dr. Whewell has admitted a special duty of Order—a duty of obeying civil law as
civil law, and only clings to the social compact because it is
an apt phrase. Again, when Dr. Whewell says, "the social-
compact is the constitution," surely this is misleading. It implies that Englishmen have consented to this constitution. Now
this can only be true if their continued residence in this country
be taken as evidence of consent, and residence can only be evidence of consent to one part of our law, if it be evidence of
consent to all parts. We have only consented to the fundamental laws of the constitution if we have consented to every statute
on the books. If our consent bar our repealing the one, it bars
our repealing the other; and yet there are some statutes which
we may certainly have a duty to repeal. There cannot be any
real danger to the great principles of our Constitution in admitting the fact that they do not depend upon consent. We do not
wish to be better Whigs than Lord Macaulay, and he treated
the original contract with contempt. There is much of truth in
what another Whig, Samuel Johnson (Coleridge's "Cobbett-
Burke") said: "To establish the throne upon a notorious untruth
is to establish it upon Mr. Milton's Vacuum, where it must fall
ten thousand fathoms deep, and know no end of falling."[123]

But turning from the conventional theory as it is in Coleridge, a self-convicted fiction, a supposition, to the great principle which Locke took from Hooker, and Rousseau from

123. *Abrogation of King James by the People of England,* etc.

Locke, we have yet to ask how far the ideal government of those who profess this theory can be called "free." It is certain that the gradual development of the conventional theory in the direction of democracy was perfectly logical; that is, that if Hooker would controvert the doctrines of Locke, he must modify some passages in his own writings, notably that passage which I have quoted; that if Locke would resist Rousseau and Tom Paine, he must contract some of his most essential propositions. Democracy seems a necessary point through which we must pass in attempting to make the consent of the governed more and more of a reality.

Since the French Revolution, the conventional theory has fallen into some discredit. Looking back now, we may say that the anti-democratic panic which Burke did much to create, was not wholly reasonable, that to it were due some of the revolutionary excesses; but below this temporary reaction there was a reasonable feeling, that the French Liberté was not a good ideal for state action. "The liberty to which Mr. Burke declared himself attached was not French Liberty,"[124] and even when it puts out of sight the horrors and absurdities of Jacobinism, English opinion is at one with Mr. Burke. The tyranny of the majority, of which De Tocqueville set the example of speaking, has become an object of dread. But still the conventional theory is popular, it crops up when men become excited; it appeared in 1832 and in 1866, it appears when any class desires to acquire a share in the government. The principal influence with which it has to contend is the influence of certain other ideals of liberty, with which it is maintained to be incompatible—for instance, religious liberty, or commercial liberty.

124. *Appeal from the New Whigs*, etc.

That there is something very plausible in calling a popular government a free government is certain. It has been so-called through ages. It is into the reasons for this that we must now enquire. Aristotle says—ὑπόθεσις μὲν οὖν τῆς δημοκρατικῆς πο-λιτείας ἐλευθερία. τοῦτο γὰρ λέγειν εἰώθασιν, ὡς ἐν μόνῃ τῇ πο-λιτείᾳ ταύτῃ μετέχοντας ἐλευθερίας.[125] He goes on to mention as one of the commonly ascribed attributes of a democracy, τὸ ζῆν ὡς βούλεταί τις.[126] Milton also, we have seen, would call a government free if it was in form "popular," though it might be forced on the nation. And certainly when we speak of a free government we do mean, among other things, that this government has in it a considerable democratic element.

Now the type of a pure democratic constitution, such as Rousseau imagined, is one in which no laws are in force save those which a majority of the citizens approve, and in which all those laws which a majority of the citizens would approve are in force. What is it that we can say of the freedom of the citizens under such a government? We have seen that Rousseau declares that if a citizen voting in a minority did by some accident get a law repealed, he would curtail his freedom, though he might thereby escape some punishment which he would otherwise have suffered. But if we construe liberty into simpler terms, if liberty means absence of restraint, how shall we say that the citizen who is always out-voted in the National Assembly is more free than the subject of an absolute monarch? We are not asking whether democracy be good or bad, but

125. [The supposition of a democratic polity is freedom. For this is what is usually said, that in this polity alone do men possess freedom.] *Pol.* vi. ii. [*Pol.* vi. i. 1317a40—not *Pol.* vi. ii.]

126. [To live as one chooses.]

simply whether it be a *free* government. If we come down to history we have many arguments on both sides, but treating the question *à priori*, should we expect to find in a democracy most freedom from restraint? τὸ ζῆν ὡς βούλεταί τις[127] is at first sight a fair description of perfect freedom. But to live as the majority wishes, seems to imply that unless we all agree, some of us must be under restraint, must be without liberty.

We may distinguish two sets of arguments on this point: (1) those which would shew that to be under the rule of the majority is perfect civil freedom; (2) those which would shew that under a popular government we are not likely to be oppressed by some of the worst forms of restraint. (1) The former class of arguments though they have been very popular, and may, in times of political strife, be very popular again, seem false. Such an argument is that of Locke, proving that we ought to be under no government except that to which we have consented, and then proving that since men are equal, and since a body cannot move in more ways than one, therefore the body politic must be concluded by the majority. Such a one is that of Rousseau, who sets up the will of the majority as an idol, and calls it *la volonté générale*. We do not think ourselves *free* when we are coerced by the will of the majority, and the *esse* of liberty is surely *percipi*. But the strangest of all such arguments is that of James Mill in his *Essay on Government*, and it is the strangest argument in that strange Essay. "The community," he says, "cannot have an interest opposite to its interests. . . . One community may intend the evil of another: never its own. This is an indubitable proposition and one of great importance." Hence he concludes that democracy is the one good form of

127. [To live as one chooses.]

government. But is it not clear that a majority may have an interest opposed to the interest of the minority? Such arguments as these are the chief evidence in favour of Comte's theory that there is a metaphysical epoch in the history of human knowledge. We have the will of all, *la volonté générale,* the interest of the community, set before us as really existing things, but when we look closer we find that they do but mean the will of a part, the interest of a part. As Kant says, the "all" which makes laws in a democracy is an "all" which is not "all."[128] In fact we have a specimen of a common logical fallacy. (2) But beneath all this there was good solid reasoning. Doubtless the conventional theory gained some of its plausibility by these identifications of the majority and the whole, by Locke's simple *id est,* and by Rousseau's elaborate sophism, but common sense is not often thus taken in; it can distinguish between τὸ ζῆν ὡς βούλεταί τις[129] and submission to a majority. The conventional theory was a great protest against certain forms of restraint, a protest which does not lose its value because the necessity of meeting the "exploded fanatics of slavery"[130] on their own ground caused it to assume a form which we cannot but think incorrect.

It was a protest against arbitrary power, or, more accurately, against the exercise of power in arbitrary ways. By arbitrary I here mean uncertain, incalculable. The exercise of power in ways which cannot be anticipated causes some of the greatest restraints, for restraint is most felt and therefore is greatest when it is least anticipated. We feel ourselves least free when we know that restraints may at any moment be placed on any

128. *Entwurf z. ewigen Frieden.*
129. [To live as one chooses.]
130. Burke.

of our actions, and yet we cannot anticipate these restraints. Hence along with the conventional theory we often find a protest against any forms of governmental restraints except such as result from known general laws. Remembering this, it is not difficult to see how "democratic" and "free" came to be thought synonymous. There has always been great practical danger of government becoming arbitrary. The Stuarts had taught us to identify monarchy and arbitrary government. The Court of Star Chamber, "a court of criminal equity," was constantly before our commonwealthsmen when they argued for democracy as for a free government. Caprice is the worst vice of which the administration of justice can be guilty; known general laws, however bad, interfere less with freedom than decisions based on no previously known rule. Where such decisions are frequent, a man can never know what liberty he has, and liberty is only valuable when we know that we have it. An arbitrary government is thus opposed to liberty, and if a democracy is less likely to be arbitrary than other governments, then it has one title to be called free. It was natural to conclude that democracy would in this sense be free. It was seen how easily a monarch could take the first steps towards the exercise of power in an arbitrary way. James and Charles had given us a lesson on this subject. And indeed it may be argued *à priori* that a democracy is less likely to exercise arbitrary power than is a monarchy. The many minds of many men check each other, one would go this way, another that, so that the steady consistency which is required of those who would exercise power arbitrarily in the face of opposition must be wanting. Strafford's "Thorough," it may be said, is not the motto of popular assemblies. We must not however go too far in this direction; we have learnt that it is possible for large masses of men to agree upon violent action, and "when they do agree, their unanimity is wonderful." Before democracies had actually been seen it was impossible to estimate the great force of contagious excitement. Here is an indication that the conventional theory, even when taken as a protest against arbitrary power, may miss its mark. If we suppose a democracy so perfectly organized that all that the majority wish to be law must be law, and that there can be no law which the majority do not approve, we fail to find in it some of those safeguards against arbitrary, incalculable, interferences with freedom, which are to be found in governments less perfectly democratic. The ideal of democratic government seems to conflict with the ideal of a government which cannot rule in an arbitrary way. Rousseau does try to insist that the popular assembly must do nothing but pass general laws, for *la volonté générale* cannot descend to particulars, but he has to make one very serious exception to this,[131] and there is no reason in his own system why he should not make more. His general line of reasoning would justify a majority of the citizens in making *privilegia* or *ex post facto* laws.

It will be noticed that the bounds which Locke would set to the acts of government are applicable to all governments monarchical or democratic. But here there is some difficulty, for apparently the popular assembly, the majority of which is in case of breach of trust by the rulers the repository of power, is not made subject to these limits. It seems to follow from this that these limits are not to be applied to a pure democratic government, which the National Assembly can, if they please, establish, for in this case the governing body is identical with that assembly whose authority apparently has no bounds. Locke, led

131. The appointment of certain persons as magistrates is a *privilegium*.

astray by his notion that the consent of the majority is in some way the consent of all, scarcely sees that there may be reasons why limits should be set to the power of a majority in a democracy.

The actual limits which Locke would set to governmental power have been already mentioned.[132] Of these, the first limits the sovereign power by making known general laws the only proper machinery of government. This is a defence against *arbitrary* power; it is a limitation of *absolute* power, making the exercise of power in arbitrary ways unconstitutional. The third again makes it wrong for the governors to tax the governed without their consent. This also is a provision against arbitrary power. The steps to arbitrary power are not open to a poor king. He must have an army, and, as Harrington says, an army is a beast with a great belly, and must be fed.[133]

On the whole we may say that the conventional theory as put forward by our early philosophers contained beneath its sweeping terms a protest against the exercise of governmental power in arbitrary ways, and a protest against any constitutional theory or "opinion of right" which allows to the ruler *absolute* power, this being *principally* objected to because it admits the exercise of *arbitrary* power.

But it was only while the conventional theory was but half developed that it was a protest against arbitrary government. In

---

132. *Civ. Gov.*, 132–141.

133. *Works.* There seems to me no absurdity in speaking of one form of government as more absolute than another, though Hobbes, Austin, and other analytical jurists think there is. That form of government is least absolute under which it may be expected that constitutional opinion, "opinion of right" (as Hume calls it), will allow to those who are ordinarily called the rulers the fewest powers.

limiting a monarchical or aristocratic government by teaching
that a certain amount of popular consent is required to make
government rightful, we may very possibly prevent such governments having resort to arbitrary measures. It seems more
easy to assume that the people have, by some original contract,
given to the rulers the power to make "promulgated, standing
laws," than that they have given the power of making *privilegia*
or *ex post facto* laws. But after the conventional theory has gone
beyond a certain point, it turns round and sets its face towards
absolute power. If the conventional theory leads to an ideally
perfect democracy—a state in which all that the majority
wishes to be law, and nothing else, is law—then it leads to a
form of government under which the arbitrary exercise of
power is most certainly possible. Thus, as it progresses, the
conventional theory seems to lose its title to be called the doctrine of civil liberty, for it ceases to be a protest against arbitrary
forms of restraint.

Those who took the road to democracy to be the road to
freedom mistook temporary means for an ultimate end. Undoubtedly, so long as there were Filmers and Heylins in the
world—so long even as there was Grotius talking about "patri-
monial" kingdoms—some steps towards democracy were steps
towards freedom, because they rendered the exercise of power
in an arbitrary way a matter of greater difficulty. But if what we
are looking for be a state in which the greatest difficulty is
placed before those who would exercise arbitrary power, we
must turn from the democratic ideal. The introduction of a
democratic element into governments has rendered us less subject to the "inconstant, uncertain, unknown will of others," not
because we are now under fewer laws to which we have not
given our consent, but because the friction of the governmental

machine has been increased, because it has become too un-
wieldy to be used in a capricious way. The exercise of arbitrary
power is least possible, not in a democracy, but in a very complicated form of government. The philosophy of "checks" has
become a little old-fashioned, and the modern protest against
it was timely. Checks cannot be created *e nihilo*, they cannot be
transplanted to foreign lands—they are only valuable when
they are the outcome of opinions of right; but when all has been
said on the other side, the fact remains that we owe our freedom
from arbitrary restraints to that elaborate constitutional theory
into which our opinions of right have, through long ages,
been crystallizing.

Here we end our long account of the conventional theory of
government. We start with Sydney's declaration that the Liberty which ought to be asserted is an exemption of all men from
all laws to which they have not given their consent. The theory
wants precision; we must know how men are to be reckoned.
Parallel with it there grows up the principle of the equality of
all men, and this is the one principle which has been used to
make the conventional theory definite. Then we start for democracy. We will make this consent more and more of a reality.
We must exclude the consent of the dead; it is the consent of
the living, those under the laws, that we require. Hobbes and
Burke try to snatch the weapon from the democrats, but in
vain, the opponents of democracy cannot use it. With Dr.
Whewell it is "a phrase," with Coleridge "a supposition." But
after all we are obliged to substitute the majority for all, our
"all" is not "all." When we have got ourselves to a perfect ideal
democracy, we find no reason for expecting *à priori* that we
shall be under fewer restraints, or fewer governmental restraints, than if we had not insisted so strongly on making the

consent of the majority a reality. We can say that a majority approves of every existing law, but we can say nothing more. We find however reason for thinking that the conventional theory in its undeveloped state did point towards freedom from a certain class of peculiarly heavy restraints, but that it did so only because it tended to complicate the machinery of government. It must be remembered that we have not been considering whether democracy be good or bad, but simply whether it be a free government, and there is small reason for calling it so.

It would now, I think, be admitted by most men that we cannot say who ought to make laws for us until we know what sort of laws ought to be made, that the best form of government is that which will best provide for the good (whatever that may mean) of its subjects, and that there are good reasons for thinking that no one form of government is the best *semper et ubique*.

But along with the protest against all laws to which the governed have not consented, and the protest against any governmental interference, save by known general laws, we find protests against laws restraining certain classes of action. The two principal classes of action for which freedom from restraint has been claimed, are the religious and the commercial.

We ought perhaps to notice separately the protests against restrictions on the publication of opinions, but it is round the publication of religious opinions that the battle has always raged. The publication of heterodox opinions has always been considered the extreme case; thus the arguments for freedom of the press are for the most part included among the arguments for religious toleration of which we must now speak.

Locke is here again the prominent figure, he has collected all the arguments for toleration into one imposing body. These arguments are so interwoven that they are somewhat difficult to analyze; what we require to know being the exact arguments for toleration, which we could address to a ruler who did not accept our religion. Some of these arguments are appeals to the religion of the ruler, others we may call non-religious, and of these we must first speak.

Locke's chief non-religious argument is, that the power committed to the magistrate extends only to the civil interests of the citizens—*i.e.* life, health, and indolency of body, and the possession of outward things; he has no power to interfere with religious matters.[134] Here and elsewhere Locke gives the weight of his name to the common theory which Warburton, following Locke, countenanced, that there are two spheres, the spiritual and the temporal, which can be definitely marked off; that within the latter the magistrate ought to be supreme, but within the former he should have no power. This however is not satisfactory. The spheres over which religion and law claim to rule really intersect. The only way in which we can draw a line between them is by making "spiritual" mean purely theoretical or speculative, and including all practice and all expression of theory under "temporal"; but this will not satisfy anyone. The religious man thinks not only that he ought to believe certain doctrines, but also that he ought to say and do certain things. If however "spiritual" include any matter of practice, then we require some criterion which shall mark off spiritual from temporal actions, and this has never been supplied. It will certainly not do to say that actions resulting from religious beliefs are spiritual, all others temporal, for we should certainly enforce the law against polygamy whether the offender were a Mormon

---

134. *Letter Concerning Toleration.* [Locke's Works, 1751, vol. II, p. 244.]

or an infidel. Sometimes Locke admits all this,[135] but the theory of the two spheres, which has since become so popular, occasionally leads him into paradoxes. He decides that a person is not to obey the law when what it enjoins appears unlawful to his conscience. Then he draws a distinction. If the law be bad, but within the proper sphere of the magistrate's power, we must disobey, but submit to punishment. If however the law "be concerning things that lie not within the verge of the magistrate's authority," men are not obliged to submit.[136] Here we have the two spheres, though Locke had acknowledged that moral actions belong to the jurisdiction of both the internal and external forum. Now to take his own case. Suppose that the magistrate, wishing his subjects to embrace a strange religion, does not insist on any change of ritual or liturgy, but on a change of conduct in regard to civil matters, believing that this change will be for the good of his subjects—*e.g.* he commands polygamy, but does not propose belief in the Book of Mormon as a test— is this command within the verge of his authority? It has to do with outward things. Most men would think resistance more excusable if the law commanded polygamy than if it commanded the use of the surplice; and yet in the former case it would, according to Locke, fall well within the sphere of the magistrate's power, in the latter case it comes under express condemnation as transgressing the proper limit. Popular opinion would not bear Locke out in drawing this line between those bad laws which do not overstep the proper limits of the magistrate's authority, and those which do so by interfering with spiritual matters. When considering whether resistance

135. Ibid., pp. 259, 261.
136. Ibid., p. 260.

would be justifiable, we do not so much inquire whether the law interferes with spiritual matters, as how bad the law is. We should justify resistance to some laws which do not, and condemn resistance to some laws which do touch spiritual matters.

The next argument is that persecution of religion must be unsuccessful. But allowing to this all its proper force, we can only say that it proves that in order to be successful our persecution must be very thorough; we must leave milder measures and resort to fire and sword. Supposing however that the ruler, to whom we address our argument, says that his religion justifies him in using all means, even the most stringent, for the coercion and conversion of heretics, what are we to say? What are we to say if the ruler hold that, whether successful or unsuccessful, he has a religious duty to abstain from tolerating heterodoxy? There seem three lines of argument open, all of which have been used by our philosophers.

(1) We may say to the magistrate that his own religion does not really permit persecution; this is the strongest argument of Milton and Locke; and we may well say that if the magistrate profess any religion which we need consider, this argument is most powerful. At any rate, if the magistrate be a Christian, this argument ought to prevail to prevent his resorting to anything worthy of the name of persecution. And now we can argue that if he is really to produce any result, he must have recourse to measures which his religion cannot approve. But Locke pushes the religious argument further. He admits that the public good (*i.e.* pleasure) is the sole end for government. He also maintains that every man has an immortal soul, capable of eternal happiness and misery, whose happiness depends upon his believing and doing those things in this life which are necessary to the obtaining of God's favour, and are prescribed

by God to that end, and the observance of these things is the highest obligation that lies upon mankind.[137] It might therefore be asked why the magistrate is to concern himself only with the temporal good of his subjects, this being so small when put beside their eternal happiness. Why should not the magistrate provide also for the latter? Locke answers, Because he cannot. Although the magistrate's opinion be sound, and the way that he appoints be truly evangelical; yet, if I be not thoroughly persuaded thereof in my own mind, there will be no safety for me in following it.[138] Now this is a distinctly religious doctrine, it asserts that right action and right belief will not profit us in another world, if they be forced upon us. This seems true, but we run into difficulties if we press the doctrine too far. We can scarcely imagine that any action or belief which is not purely voluntary can, from a religious point of view, be considered meritorious. This would lead us to say that no beliefs which are the result of the force of education or custom can be meritorious; and yet most men would say that they ought to take some means to spread their religion. This duty may not be deducible from a duty to secure our neighbour's everlasting happiness, which may only be attainable by his own voluntary efforts, and yet it may be a plain duty. Thus it might be urged, in answer to Locke, that by using force to compel my neighbour to accept true religion, I do not make him more virtuous in the sight of God, but I do fulfill a plain duty. Perhaps the ordinary way of drawing a line is saying that I ought not to make my neighbour a hypocrite, but that, short of this, my religion obliges me to use all means to convert him. Thus, taking the common view

137. Ibid., p. 259.
138. Ibid., p. 253.

of religion, there seem sufficient reasons why a man, be he a magistrate or not, should refrain from the coarser forms of persecution. Persecution by fire and sword, or by imposing disabilities, converts no one without making him a hypocrite; but those more delicate forms of compulsion which consist in giving advantages by state machinery to what we consider true religion, do not seem condemnable.

(2) We may argue that the ruler could not prove the truth of his religion without first setting up some standard of right and wrong independent of that religion. Unfortunately, Locke was one of the few philosophers to whom this line of argument was not open. But if we accept our religion because we first accept some ethical creed, then we cannot say that we ought to enforce any commands of that religion which are flagrantly at variance with those moral doctrines on which the proof of our religion rests.

The third argument may be for a moment postponed. Here we will refer to Coleridge's criticism of Locke. "It would," he says, "require stronger arguments than any which I have heard as yet, to prove that men have not a right, involved in an imperative duty, to deter those under their control from teaching or countenancing doctrines which they believe to be damnable, and even to punish with death those who violate such prohibition. I am sure that Bellarmine would have had small difficulty in turning Locke round his finger's end upon this ground. . . . The only true argument as it seems to me, apart from Christianity, for a discriminating toleration, is that it is of no use to attempt to stop heresy or schism by persecution, unless perhaps it be conducted upon the plan of direct warfare and massacre."[139] This is in the main quite true. Locke's argument

139. *Table Talk,* 3rd Jan., 1834.

about the two spheres is faulty, and having merged ethics in religion, he has nothing left to appeal to but the religion of the ruler; all he can say to the persecuting prince is that Christianity does not permit persecution. If the prince were not a Christian, Locke must content himself with saying that Christianity is "reasonable," and that therefore the prince ought to be a Christian. But Locke has one argument in reserve, and this is the really important argument, and this Coleridge fails to see. It must now be stated.

(3) Milton in the *Areopagitica* argues that the suppression of unlicensed books is "the stop of truth." Now what does this imply? Why, that governors cannot be certain that they know what the truth is. The *Areopagitica* sounds like a prolonged echo of Gamaliel's words, "Refrain from these men, and let them alone, . . . lest haply ye be found even to fight against God." This will bear translating from the religious language; it is advice not to persecute because we may be persecuting the truth. This argument is not put very prominently forward by Locke, but it runs through his whole work. Suppose now that we argue before the persecuting prince that (though, if he be absolutely certain of the truth of his religion, that religion alone can set bounds to his persecution) he ought not to be absolutely certain of his religion; that the evidence does not justify absolute certainty; we throw him back upon some independent moral creed. Perhaps he has no such creed to fall back upon? Then our case is hopeless, but at any rate he can no longer say that it is his religion which obliges him to persecute; if he will justify his acts at all, he must justify them by some other standard than his religion; if he will not justify them, argument is obviously thrown away. If however we can get him to accept any known ethical creed, then we have ground for a fresh plea for toleration.

Do we then say that it is the duty of rulers to doubt their religion, to think that other religions may be equally true? Not quite. It was not the least of Butler's services to English philosophy that he insisted on probability being the real guide of our lives. Now probability essentially admits of degrees, and it is possible that we may hold some opinion to be sufficiently probable to justify us in acting on it in some cases, though not in all. We may have such a degree of assurance of the truth of some doctrine, that any known moral creed would oblige us to guide our more private actions by it, and yet would oblige us to refrain from forcing it upon our neighbours. We see indications that such thoughts as this have been present to the minds of those who have pleaded for toleration. This will serve to explain and *justify* the fact that the pleaders for toleration limit the field to which toleration is applicable, a fact otherwise only explicable by cynicism. We find that Milton and Locke will tolerate those opinions which seem to them just possibly true. Milton stops short at "popery and open superstition . . . that also which is impious or evil absolutely either against faith or manners."[140] Locke stops short at popery and atheism.[141] Mill does not stop short at all. The question which these philosophers asked themselves was—Can the suppression of this or that opinion conceivably be "the stop of truth"? If so, this is one reason against any attempt at suppression. If once it be admitted that there is considerable chance of compulsion being exercised to promote not what is right, but what is wrong, then the arguments of Milton, Locke, and Mill become really forcible, and Bellarmine could scarcely make such short work of Locke

140. *Areop.*
141. *Letter Concerning Toleration,* pp. 260–261.

as Coleridge imagined; for the persecutor requires it to be granted that if we accept a doctrine as true enough for some purposes, we must accept it as true enough for all purposes. But this is just what the reader of Butler will never grant.

Toleration is often pleaded for on too weak grounds. We can scarcely ask the ruler not to interfere, without suggesting to him that there is a chance of his own opinions being wrong. The really convincing part of Mill's argument is that in which he shows how often intolerance has been on the side of falsehood. Scepticism or doubt is the legitimate parent of toleration.

The opinions of so essentially religious a philosopher as Coleridge on this point have a peculiar value. If the passage just quoted from his *Table Talk* stood alone, we might suppose that he preferred the conclusions of Bellarmine to those of Locke, but this is the very reverse of the truth; he was prepared to go as far as Locke, though for different reasons. He speaks of himself as "I who have . . . so earnestly contended that religion cannot take on itself the character of law without *ipso facto* ceasing to be religion, and that law could neither recognize the obligations of religion for its principles, nor become the pretended guardian and protector of the faith, without degenerating into inquisitorial tyranny."[142] If we put this passage by the side of the other, we shall come to the conclusion that Coleridge held that it is Christianity itself which forbids law to recognize the obligations of religion as its principles. This, no doubt, was his opinion, and it adds one more to the pleas for toleration. Coleridge certainly held that the outward object of virtue is the greatest producible sum of happiness of all men.[143] Law can

142. *Church and State*, Advertisement.
143. *Aids to Reflection*, Prud. Aph. 11. Comment.

only deal with what is outward, thus the greatest happiness of all men must be the end at which all law should aim.[144] At the same time he will not hear of Utilitarianism in private ethics, because Utilitarianism defeats its own end, because before we can attain the outward object of virtue, we must have an inward virtuous impulse which religion alone can supply. But religion in politics, like Utilitarianism in ethics, defeats its own end, for the outward object of virtue alone comes within the purview of the law. This will explain why it is that Coleridge directs his attack against Paley rather than Bentham; he did not object to Utilitarianism as a principle of legislation, he did object to making the future life a matter of calculation. Bentham was incomplete, Paley was wrong.

This theory helps Coleridge to cut a difficult knot. Warburton, holding that the State ought to form an alliance with *some* Church, pronounces that the Church which should be chosen, is that to which the mass of the subjects belong. With this Mr. Gladstone expressed himself dissatisfied; the prince, he thought, is in duty bound to give every advantage to *his own* religion.[145]

Coleridge, like Warburton and Mr. Gladstone, would have an established Church, but he contends that religion itself obliges us to accept expedience as the measure for law, law must not recognize the obligations of religion for its principles, it must when treating of religion consider only its "this-worldian" effects. The national Church is not established to teach religion "in the spiritual sense of the word, as understood in reference

144. *The Friend,* Essay III.
145. *The State in Relation to the Church,* ch. ii. § 16.

to a future state."[146] It is merely a "blessed accident" that the national clerisy can be the teachers of religion in an exalted, spiritual sense; this is not what they are paid for; they are paid for making men better citizens, neighbours, subjects; their "this-worldian" utility is the measure of their services, and those whoever they be who can best perform the function of making the people good, in a Utilitarian sense, ought to be members of the national clerisy.

Now, if Coleridge's be the true Christian view of the matter, there seems to be a chance of reconciling those who are at issue about the duties of the State as regards religious bodies. Bentham and the Oxford tractators have scarce any ground in common, Bentham and Coleridge are agreed about a first principle.

There have never been wanting arguments for religious toleration, for Christianity itself was a standing protest against persecution, but when we turn from religious liberty to commercial liberty, the case is different. As long as the real operation of commerce was wholly misconceived, the now common arguments for *laisser faire* could not be brought forward. Some conception of the way in which wealth is produced and distributed must exist, before these arguments can become evident.

The immense difficulties which King William's government had to overcome in their reform of the coinage gave birth to modern political economy; the supply was occasioned by a demand. The action of money and the benefits of trade had already been the subject of speculation in Greece, in England, above all in Italy; but the first sketch of the science as it at present exists is, I believe, due to Locke, whose services in the mat-

146. *Church and State.*

ter of the currency the government had been wise enough to secure. As might be expected, Locke was not content until he had penetrated to first principles. In his *Considerations of the Lowering of Interest* he incidentally lays down twenty-one propositions which might be placed as headings to the various chapters of the *Wealth of Nations*.

We may notice, that directly the distribution of wealth becomes the subject of searching speculation, the protest against legislative interference with commerce at once begins. Locke argued, in the way now familiar, that it is futile to meddle with the rate of interest. It is not however true to say with Macaulay[147] that Locke went farther than Smith, and anticipated Bentham. No, the honour of having been the first consistent opponent of the usury laws fairly belongs to Bentham. In fact, this is a most striking triumph of systematic over unsystematic Utilitarianism. Locke, Smith, Paley, all condemn the principle of the usury laws, but they are not prepared to recommend their abolition; they catch at some straw of popular prejudice. Usurers must not have a monopoly,[148] projectors should not be favoured,[149] governments should be able to borrow at a low rate.[150] Bentham's searching analysis, his ceaseless question, why? swept such arguments aside. It was because he was determined to call no law good if it did not produce more pleasure than pain, that he was able to convert Adam Smith, to win exaggerated praises from so unsympathetic a critic as Mackin-

147. *Hist. Engl.*, ch. xxi.
148. *Locke's Works*, vol. ii, p. 33.
149. *Wealth of Nations*, Bk. ii, ch. iv.
150. *Mor. and Pol. Phil.*, ii. x.

tosh,[151] and, as Hallam[152] says, to convince the thinking part of mankind.

To return. Hume's economic essays must also have influenced Adam Smith; whatever Hume touched he illuminated. But when all is said, the *Wealth of Nations* is the first systematic book on what is now called political economy, it is also the first powerful plea for commercial freedom. The difficulty of the work which Smith set himself to do can scarcely be overrated. A society founded on custom had given way to a society founded on competition, but the operations of the new economic force had never been explained. Even Bacon's mind could not penetrate the mists which hung over the taking of usury.[153] Here also fiction had to be expelled by science.

Adam Smith wrote the *Wealth of Nations* in part fulfilment of a promise to write a discourse "on the general principles of law and government." His purpose was to shew what laws ought to be made concerning "police, revenue, and arms."[154] Thus his conception of political economy obviously differs from that of Ricardo and his followers. Political economy is now looked upon as a science, teaching what is, or what in certain circumstances will be, the way in which wealth is produced and distributed. Doubtless it is well to separate the consideration of what is, and what will be, from the consideration of what ought to be, such a separation is dictated by logical convenience; but if this separation is to be made, it should be made consistently,

151. *Hist. Eth. Phil.* (3rd ed.), p. 240.
152. *Hist. Lit.*, vol. IV, ch. iv.
153. *Essays: Of Usury.*
154. Comp. *Moral Sentiments,* VII. iv., with preface to 6th edition of that work.

and it never is made consistently. Even the scientific Ricardo
breaks off his almost algebraic speculations to tell us what is the
only justification for the poor laws.[155] As long as we are careful
to keep ourselves from appealing to any ideal, as long as we
neither justify nor condemn, there seem good reasons for separating the science of political economy from the general science
of society, sociology, or ethology as it is called. The best reason
is, that the former exists, that it has done good work, discovered
valuable truths, truths verified by experience, and that there is
no cause for thinking that its work is done, while on the other
hand, we know little more than the name of sociology. We may
add that even when a social science becomes a reality there still
may be room for a deductive science inquiring into the effects
of the wealth-getting motives. As long as we carefully exclude
the ideal, the moral, and concern ourselves only with what is,
and what will be, there is little difficulty in answering the objections of Comte and Coleridge; we merely appeal to experience;
we say, for instance, that the theory of foreign exchanges, as
taught by Mill, really does explain those complicated phenomena of the money market which were previously inexplicable.
But if once we begin to say how the production and distribution of wealth *ought to be* carried on we can no longer confine
our attention to facts about wealth. We have to decide how
far wealth is desirable, we have to compare wealth with other
desirable objects. We cannot say that *laisser faire* should be
our rule until we are agreed upon subjects which are quite alien
to the science of wealth. Our economists should make their
choice, either they must give up talking about what ought to
be, or they must take into consideration ethical and political

155. *Pol. Econ.*, ch. v.

doctrines on which the methods of the science of wealth throw no light. Of all our writers on political economy the most successful have been those who have most constantly kept in view the fact that when the economist begins to justify and condemn, he has passed the bounds of his own special science, he has become a moralist, and must behave as such. Aristotle introduces what he has to say about how men ought to act in distributing wealth, into the middle of that book of his Ethics which deals with the virtue of justice. Sir A. Grant thinks that to make political economy a part of morals is a mistake we should never now fall into.[156] But surely the Greek philosopher is more right than his critic. If we say that wealth ought to be distributed in this or that way, we do set forth a distinctly moral theory, a theory which we are bound to defend in the lists of ethics. No amount of truths about what is, or what in certain circumstances will be, can make one truth as to what ought to be. Therefore we should object to the practice of some of our economists, who seem to press upon us the doctrine that the State ought not to interfere with commerce, as if this was deducible from the doctrine that all men try to buy as cheaply and sell as dearly as possible.[157]

The reasons which Mill has given for separating political economy from ethology appear perfectly valid, as long as political economy keeps clear of what ought to be;[158] but there is no reason for thinking that the ethics of the distribution of wealth

156. *Essays,* App. C.

157. Specimens of such a procedure could be extracted from several popular manuals; they go far to justify Coleridge's opinion that Political Economy is solemn humbug. (*Table Talk,* March 17th, 1833.)

158. *Logic,* VI. ix. 3.

can be separated from general ethics. Adam Smith and Mill have recognized this more clearly than many of their fellows, and they have their reward.

Now to consider the arguments in favour of commercial freedom. The first and most popular is based on a supposed harmony of economic interests. It is said that every man best provides for the economic interests of the whole by providing for his own economic interests. Adam Smith started this argument. "As every individual therefore endeavours as much as he can both to employ his capital in the support of domestic industry, and so to direct that industry that its produce may be of the greatest value, every individual necessarily labours to render the annual revenue of the society as great as he can, . . . he is in this, as in many other cases, led by an invisible hand to promote an end which was no part of his intention. Nor is it always the worse for the society that it was no part of it. By pursuing his interest he frequently promotes that of the society more effectually than when he intends to promote it." First let us notice the "invisible hand"; these words point to the source of Adam Smith's ethics, the optimist school of Hobbes' opponents, those who thought that true self-love and social are the same, that it was derogatory to the honour of God Almighty that he should have left his master-workmanship Man in a state of war.[159] This is not unimportant, for this belief in a providence directing our selfish aims to social good has formed one of the strongest arguments for *laisser faire*. But passing this by, it will be seen that Adam Smith's belief in the harmony of economic interests did not carry him very far. In one place he admits that the interest of the capitalist is not consonant with the interests of the land-

159. *Clarendon's Reply to Hobbes.*

lord and the labourer.[160] His grounds for thinking that the interests of the landlord are more consonant with those of the labourers than with those of the capitalist would now be considered unsound; but this admission of a partial dissonance is extremely damaging to the popular argument for *laisser faire*. The invisible hand has after all failed to harmonize our economic interests. It cannot be too much insisted on that Adam Smith threw really very little weight on these *à priori* arguments about harmony, in which Bastiat delights; they are not essential parts of his argument against the mercantile theory, they are *obiter dicta*. The real leading argument is: you say that your system of interference enriches the country, by bringing into it gold and silver; I will shew that gold and silver are not peculiarly desirable forms of wealth, that your system checks the growth of what you will admit is real wealth, that it does not even attain its own worthless object. Adam Smith's argument is for the most part *ad homines*, his opponents justified a meddling policy as productive of wealth, and Adam Smith completely refuted this justification. But what is the really powerful part of the refutation? Not the assertion about an invisible hand, but the detailed proof that all the restraints on free trade imposed or suggested had failed, and must fail. When we further notice that Adam Smith's assertions about the harmony of interests are chiefly meant to show that all men have an interest (not necessarily an equal interest) in the freedom of international trade, when we notice that in the conclusion of his first book in a sort of summary of its results, he warns us that the judgment of capitalists about the interests of society is to be taken with reserve, as it is warped by their judgment of their own

160. *Wealth of Nations*, i. xi. Conclusion.

interests, we cannot appeal to him as the father of those who see nothing but harmonies in political economy. What would Bastiat say to this: the proposals made by capitalists come from "an order of men whose interest is never exactly the same with that of the public, who have generally an interest to deceive and even to oppress the public"? Above all, Adam Smith certainly did not believe that the economic interests of a nation are always harmonious with its other interests.

Have the additions to political economy made since Smith's day shewn our economic interests to be more harmonious than he thought them? Surely the reverse. Malthus has pointed to a social force which, since it plays a great part in the distribution of wealth, may be called economic, and which would seem to cause a divergence between the interests of various classes of society. It is said that as a fact men do go on increasing their numbers until there is always a large class who can barely obtain the necessaries of life. Is it to the capitalist's economic interest that this should not be so? The fact should be admitted. It is distinctly to the economic interest of the capitalist that there should be as many people as possible willing to work for as small wages as possible, always provided that the breed of labourers be not seriously damaged by overcrowding and insufficient food. Is this a new harmony? It was a sound instinct that made those who hoped for the improvement ("melioration" was the word then) of mankind by trusting to the play of selfish but harmonious instincts to talk about "godless Malthusianism." Malthus did strike a blow at the eighteenth century conception of God, the Being who turns selfishness into benevolence.

What is the greatest discovery of modern economy? Most men would say Ricardo's *Law of Rent*. This again shews an ob-

vious discord between the interests of the landlords and those
of the labouring classes. It is to the landlord's economic interest
that population should not be diminished. Bastiat saw the want
of harmony here; he denied the truth of Ricardo's law. He
might as well have denied the truth of Euclid. Again, no
amount of the special pleading, of which he was a master, can
get over this simple fact. It is distinctly contrary to the economic interests of the capitalist that labourers should become
any richer than they now are, their numbers remaining constant. Whatever view we may take of ethics, surely there is a
strong *primâ facie* case for saying with Carlyle that *laissez faire*
and Malthus positively must part company?[161] But only a *primâ
facie* case. The main argument of the *Wealth of Nations* remains
to this day a valid reason for leaving trade free, and the main
argument is that interference only makes bad worse. This has
been forcibly repeated by post-Malthusian economists, who
have argued that our present system of private property, freedom of contract, considerable testamentary powers, is in its
broad outlines more likely to produce the happiness of mankind than any other legislative system yet sketched out. The
argument is, briefly, that in our present system legislative interference is nearly at a minimum; that any other system would
require constant and meddling interferences; that such interferences themselves cause pain; that such interferences would
be futile, the economic forces with which they have to contend
being too powerful to be turned from their course; that self-
reliance would be destroyed. But after all, the most powerful
argument is that based on the ignorance, the necessary ignorance, of our rulers. The evil of governmental interference var-

161. *Chartism.*

ies with the probability of the government being wrong, and
until political economy is a very much more perfect science
than there seems any chance of its being for a long time yet, we
may fairly say that there is great probability that any governmental interference with commerce would be made on mistaken grounds, and would defeat its own end. Adam Smith
shewed by the method of exhaustive failures that legislative interferences with foreign trade have been hurtful or futile, and
his followers have successfully shewed that the same may be
said of interferences with commercial transactions in general.

It is very necessary however that it should be seen that the
principle of *laisser faire* does not rest on a belief in the harmony
of interests. If such were the case, it would be possible to say
that since a man will best consult the economic interests of the
community by attending to no one's interest but his own, to
buy cheap and sell dear is the whole economic duty of man. It
is this supposed corollary that excites opposition to the principle, it is thought that the economic "Laissez faire" involves
the Rabelaisian "Fay ce que voudras."[162] That this is no necessary deduction, when the principle is placed on a sound foundation, will readily be seen. That the difficulty of opposing
powerful economic forces, the danger of giving wide powers to
government, the necessary ignorance of our governors, make it
inadvisable that law should meddle with the settlement of
wages and prices, is no reason why the individual should forget,
in the distribution of his wealth, that his own economic interests are frequently directly opposed to the economic interests
of others.

Adam Smith has remarked that the laws made about religion

162. [Do what you will.]

and commerce have been peculiarly bad, and we may notice that laws on these two subjects were the first laws condemned as essentially going beyond the proper province of law. Religion and commerce seem ideas widely removed from each other, but yet in the eye of the statesman they have points in common. (1) It is difficult to make laws about them which shall not be futile. It is so easy to introduce and circulate both smuggled goods and smuggled opinions. The forces with which such laws have to contend are the most powerful forces of human nature. (2) Interference on the wrong side may produce the worst effects; it may bring starvation, it may be "the stop of truth." (3) It is very probable that the interference will be on the wrong side. There are no subjects with which the statesman has to deal, the logic of which is so elaborate and so difficult. This last reason, though it is not often expressly insisted on (we do not like to confess our own ignorance, or impress on others their ignorance when we have nothing to substitute for it) is really all-important. The statesman has to consider the good he may do by interfering on the right side, the evil he may do by interfering on the wrong side, and also the probability of his knowing which the right side is. The most convincing pleas for *laisser faire*, and the most convincing pleas for religious toleration, are those which insist *à priori* on the great "probable error" of any opinions on matters of religion, and matters of political economy, and those which relate *à posteriori* the history of the well-intentioned failures of wise and good men.

To return for a moment to democracy, the connection between the liberty of democracy and commercial liberty does not seem strong. We should say that there is no reason why a monarch should not see the folly of protection as soon as would the majority of the nation; his interests on this point may well be at one with those of his subjects. The cases of France under Napoleon III, and of the United States at the present time shew that any connection which exists is but weak. Nor does it appear that democracies are peculiarly likely to be tolerant in matters of religion. Hobbes certainly thought otherwise; indeed it is not improbable that a belief that an absolute monarchy would allow the greatest freedom of thought, was the motive power in making this bitter enemy of the clergy of all confessions an apologist for the royal martyr. However, it seems just plausible to say that though contagious enthusiasm may make a democracy intolerant, it will interfere first on this side, then on that, until successive failures teach it wisdom.

We must pass from these special cases of laws condemned as violations of liberty, to the more general question of how we are to know those laws which violate the desirable liberty. First let us mention one or two definitions of liberty. Harrington[163] says "the liberty of a commonwealth is the empire of the laws," not the laws made by consent, but simply "the laws." Liberty is here the absence of government by arbitrary methods. Next we have another group of definitions. Rutherforth, a commentator on Grotius, says that civil liberty is "as much liberty as is consistent with the obligation of the social compact"[164]—but of the social compact we have already said enough. Blackstone takes civil liberty to be "natural liberty so far restrained by human laws (and no further) as is necessary and expedient for the general advantage of the public."[165] With Paley, civil liberty is "the being restrained by no law but what in a greater degree con-

163. *Works*, p. 45.
164. *Institutes*, II. viii. 7.
165. *Comment.*, I. i.

duces to the public welfare."[166] But these two last definitions amount merely to this, civil liberty is the absence of *bad* laws. Is it possible to go beyond this, to say not that liberty is the absence of bad laws, but that some laws are bad because they interfere with liberty? Let us examine the now common arguments against the multiplication of laws—arguments now common but once rare. Harrington is one of the few of our earlier philosophers who has said, "the best rule as to your laws is that they be few."[167] Milton objected to "the old entanglement of iniquity, their gibrish laws,"[168] rather because they hide the law of God than because they interfere with Liberty.

(1) Bad laws may do a great deal of harm. This argument is independent of the Benthamite doctrine hereafter to be referred to, that all laws being restraints are painful. This argument is open to moralists of all schools, for bad laws will give pain, violate conscience, contradict true propositions; we can use what phrase we please. We only speak of the evils of *bad* laws.

(2) Laws are likely to be bad. The probable error of even well-intentioned statesmen is great. Here again all moralists can unite. We cannot trust our rulers' knowledge of right and wrong, whether that knowledge come from experience or from intuition. Perhaps however the argument is most forcible in the mouths of those who believe that calculation of consequences is necessary.

The great difference between Mill's *Essay on Liberty* and earlier writings on the same subject is, that Mill resists the pre-

166. *Mor. and Pol. Phil.*, vi. x.
167. *Works*, p. 60.
168. *Tenure of Kings.*

sumption that uniformity of action is desirable. As long as the influence of Locke was dominant, so long the convenient psychological assumption that men are by nature very much alike, ran through our political philosophy. Now if the characters of men be alike, then when men are placed in the same circumstances they ought to do the same things; this is the fundamental assumption of all moral philosophers. If men be very much alike, then uniformity of conduct is desirable; there is a presumption that two men placed in the same external circumstances ought to act in the same way. This presumption fails if, as modern science teaches us, we are not endowed with equal faculties at starting. Mill broke away from the eighteenth-century tradition; self-development "in its richest variety" was not an ideal for the followers of Locke, for there was a presumption against variety. The resistance of this presumption gave new force to the argument that laws will probably be bad. Law can only deal with externals, it can scarcely concern itself with character and the more reason there is for insisting on the character of the agent as a necessary element in our consideration of the rightness of the action, the less reason is there for thinking external uniformity of action desirable.

We may add that probability being the guide of life, the statesman is not obliged to assume that because he believes some doctrine to be true enough for some purposes, he ought to believe that it is true enough for all purposes.

(3) Bentham says, "every restriction imposed upon liberty is subject to be followed by a natural sentiment of pain, greater or less. . . . He who proposes a coercive law ought to be ready to prove not only that there is a specific reason in favour of it, but that this reason is of more weight than the general reason

against every such law."[169] This is certainly a correct deduction from Utilitarianism. To restrain or thwart a man is always to give him pain. It must be doubtful how far anti-Utilitarian moralists would admit that this raised any presumption against a new law. Sometimes they speak as if the only desirable freedom was to be found in right action. "Was ist die freieste Freiheit? Recht zu thun."[170] This leads us to look upon those laws which oblige us to act morally, as not really restraints; they do but bind us to a service which is perfect freedom. Hence there might be some difference on this point. But if we put the question—Is the pain caused by legal restraint in itself an evil? would it not be desirable to lessen this pain, if we could, by other means secure the performance of the moral action? we should probably get but one answer. But, as a fact, this argument has come principally from professed Utilitarians. They can look at absence of restraint as *per se* desirable, for it is the absence of a certain class of pains. So the Utilitarian, at any rate, is not compelled to answer the question "Who is at liberty to do what, and from what restraint is he liberated?"[171] before he expresses a desire for liberty. He wishes for freedom from the pain of restraint, just as he wishes for freedom from the pain of gout. It may be well for other people, or even for himself, that he should be under restraint, just as it may be well for them that he should have the gout; but looked at by itself and apart from its consequences, the Utilitarian must hold that both for himself and for others, freedom from restraint is desirable.

169. *Treatise* (Dumont), p. 94.
170. [What is the freest freedom? To do right.] Goethe. *Egmont.*
171. J. F. Stephen, *Liberty*, etc., p. 175.

With such materials as these, Mill attempted to establish a doctrine of Liberty as a middle axiom of Utilitarianism. He attempted to obtain a principle by reference to which we might condemn laws as interfering with Liberty, without ascending in every case to the supreme rule of Benthamism. In his *Essay on Liberty* he says, "The object of this essay is to assert one very simple principle as entitled to govern absolutely the dealings of society with the individual in the way of compulsion and control, whether the means used be physical force in the form of legal penalties or the moral coercion of public opinion. That principle is, that the sole end for which mankind are warranted, individually or collectively, in interfering with the liberty of action of any of their number, is self-protection."[172] This seems quite opposed to what Mill had said in his *Political Economy*, namely, that the functions of government are not capable of being circumscribed by those very definite lines of demarcation which, in the considerateness of popular discussion, it is attempted to draw round them. There, he says, that to afford protection against force and fraud is too narrow a field. "There is a multitude of cases in which governments, with general approbation, assume powers and execute functions for which no reason can be assigned, except the simple one that they conduce to general convenience."[173] Nor can I think that the former passage was intended to over-rule the latter, for in the very *Essay on Liberty* it is admitted that "for such actions as are prejudicial to the interests of others the individual is accountable, and may be subjected either to social or to legal punishment, if society is of opinion that the one or the other is requisite for its protec-

172. Ibid., ch. i.
173. *Pol. Econ.*, v. i. 2. There are even stronger expressions, too long to quote.

tion."[174] In this last passage the definiteness of "self-protection" vanishes. Society may use coercion in order to protect itself against actions prejudicial to its interests. In fact, we have to extend self-protection until it means protection from any pain. The ordinary use of words scarcely permits this. Society could scarcely justify compulsory education by the plea of self-protection.

Bentham said, "The care of his enjoyments ought to be left almost entirely to the individual. The principal function of government is to guard against pains."[175] The doctrine of Mill's essay (expanded, as it must be, so as to make self-protection mean protection against any pain) agrees with the passage, only the words "almost" and "principally" must be omitted. It is however doubtful whether the Utilitarian can spare these words. Mill certainly would not have objected to giving compulsory powers of purchase to railway companies, and yet railways rather increase our pleasures than diminish our pains. This is but a type of a large class of cases, many of which are expressly admitted in the *Political Economy* as being cases where interference is justifiable.

Nor is the Utilitarian justified in saying that we ought never to interfere with an individual for his own good. We should probably push away a blind man from the brink of a precipice. Neither can it be said that we may only interfere in these cases when a man is going to do what he does not want to do: this principle would be too elastic, for the drunkard does not want *delirium tremens*. The reason why we should employ force in the one case and not in the other, is not that in the one case the

174. Ibid., ch. v.
175. *Treatise*, p. 95.

pain is not desired, while in the other it is, but rather that we, the interferers, are more certain of the impending evil in the one than in the other, and are far more likely to prevent the evil at a small expense of pain.

Thus, though Mill has done much towards making the arguments for non-interference more complete, he has not been able to establish a precise middle axiom of Utilitarianism. The doctrine of his Political Economy, that no reason can be given for a multitude of governmental interferences, "except the simple one, that they conduce to general convenience," must be taken as the last word of Benthamism on the subject of Liberty.

All therefore that we get from Utilitarianism by way of a protest for liberty is the assertion that all restraint is painful, and therefore *primâ facie* bad. Besides this we have much proof that interferences on the wrong side may do much evil, and that it is far from improbable that interferences will be on the wrong side. This being so, we can scarcely make the minimization of restraint our political ideal. One of the strongest reasons for non-interference is one which we may hope will rather lose than gain in strength—we may hope that the "probable error" of legislation may in time be diminished.

There is however a newer philosophy which makes absence of restraint its ideal. Mr. Spencer's doctrines are in many ways thoroughly post-Coleridgean, but something may be said of their historical origin. Coleridge, in his sketch of political philosophy, mentions three systems: (1) that of Hobbes, based on fear; (2) that of expediency, to which Coleridge professed himself attached; (3) that of the pure reason. In his description of the last he refers to Rousseau, but the doctrines as he sets them forth are more German than French in their form—they are more the doctrines of Kant than of Rousseau. The ideal of this system was, he says, that legislation should remove all obstructions to free action, and do nothing more. "The greatest possible happiness of a people is not according to this system the object of a governor, but to preserve the freedom of all by coercing within the requisite bounds the freedom of each."[176] Such words are familiar to us now. Coleridge himself had been an ardent admirer of this system—he had founded on it his scheme of Pantisocracy; to the end he treated it with regretful respect; but he found himself obliged to abandon and refute it, because he thought that it logically led him to absurd conclusions. It was too good for this world; it is "under any form impracticable"; an attempt to realize it "would necessarily lead to general barbarism and the most grinding oppression." Coleridge's opinion is all the more valuable because he cannot be charged with empiricism—he loved whatever belonged to the pure reason.

Mr. Spencer desires the minimization of *all* restraints. From this he passes to the recommendation of the abolition of all government as an ultimate ideal. Now here we do at last see the end of the conventional theory. We saw how when Rousseau had established his democracy, he was reduced to a sophism to prove that men, when punished, have given their consent to be punished. This could not last; if we are to be under no laws save those to which we have consented (and Sydney says that this ought to be the case), surely we ought to be able to annul a law by withdrawing our consent. We must make consent more real yet; we must pass Rousseau and join Mr. Spencer. Mr. Spencer has really a strong historical case. He might say that Hooker, Milton, Locke, Sydney, Rousseau, have laid down a maxim

176. *The Friend,* Essay IV.

which leads to his theory, that Hobbes, Burke, and Conservatives in general have been obliged to invent a spurious imitation, that Coleridge and Whewell cannot bring themselves to quite abandon his principle. But then there is Hume, Bentham, Mill, and Coleridge (when he can forget his first love); what of these? Mr. Spencer tries to fuse his system with Utilitarianism. If we will but leave action unrestrained, nature will do the rest, and will produce a race of men perfectly happy, because perfectly adapted to their environment; thus a scientifically sanctioned process is substituted for the Benthamite rule of thumb. Unfortunately, Mr. Spencer refuses to deal with "moral therapeutics"—which are what the world must be concerned with for the next few million years—and constructs a philosophy of rights for men adapted to their environment; so it is hard to say what chance he has of converting the Utilitarian from his "moral infidelity."[177]

In order to gain over the Utilitarian he must shew not only that to set about minimizing restraints will ultimately produce a state of perfect bliss, but that, taking into consideration the present as well as the future, and properly discounting the future, the happiness of mankind would be added to by every diminution of restraint. This may be the case, and yet it will be difficult to prove that it is so, unless one simple proposition be true, namely, that each individual's happiness varies inversely with the restraints which he is under. If this be not true it does not indeed follow that Mr. Spencer's rule may not be the best method of obtaining Bentham's object; it may be that though the greatest freedom of all is the greatest happiness of all, yet the freest individual is not the happiest. But if this be the case

177. *Social Statics*, ch. xx.

we can scarcely hope to shew the harmony between Bentham's Supreme Rule and the maxim of Liberty, the proof is quite beyond any methods at our command. And it certainly is not true that the individual's happiness varies with his freedom from restraints due to other men. From such restraints Alexander Selkirk was perfectly free, and yet he was not happy.

This being so, an empirical proof that the minimization of restraints produces the maximum of happiness seems impossible. As to the scientific proof from adaptation, it only shews that at some future time there will be a race of completely happy men, it cannot shew that the Utilitarian should sacrifice the happiness of present generations to the happiness of future, and so we most certainly require a scheme of moral therapeutics, of ethics for imperfect beings. Lastly, there is the theological argument from design, and this seems stronger. Systems of absolute rights require such a theological basis as Locke relied on. But this is scarcely cogent when we substitute the "Unknowable" of the *First Principles* for the "God" of the *Social Statics.*

If with Kant we attach some supreme value to the action of free will, thinking it the only good *per se,* it is natural to make the minimization of restraints on free will the supreme principle of law; but we cannot yet say that this is compatible with Utilitarianism, with which, very prudently, Kant will have nothing to do. His doctrine appears to be that since the law cannot deal with anything but externals, and therefore is no judge of the internal freedom of an action, the minimization of restraints on *all* action is the proper jural means to the minimization of restraints on free action. The problem therefore is the minimization of all restraints (or of all restraints caused by human action) by law. But every law implies restraint. Therefore we have to get rid of greater restraints by imposing smaller restraints. To do this we must have some measure of the greatness of a restraint. What shall this be? We look in vain for an answer. There is only one measure which seems possible, and that is the greatness of the pain caused by the restraint. So our rule becomes—Minimize the pain of restraint. Thus even the purest Kantian who takes the analysis of the idea of freedom as the means of discovering what law ought to be has to admit a calculus of pleasure and pain into his politics. This should be remembered when the philosophers who would deduce Ideal Law from the maxim of Liberty assert as against the Utilitarian that such a calculus is impossible. If it be impossible we have not yet found a first principle of Politics.

Equality

Equality has never been so universally accepted an ideal of politics as Liberty. Still, it would on all hands be admitted that "Equality before the law" is good. We require—(1) an impartial administration of justice, and (2) impartial laws—that is, laws making no distinctions save such as are necessary consequences of the principle according to which all laws should be framed.[178] But we must pass to more controverted matter, to the claims which have been made in favour of equality of political power, and equality of property.

The premises from which Locke would deduce a system of morality are: the existence of a Supreme Being, infinite in power, goodness, and wisdom, whose workmanship we are, and on whom we depend; and of ourselves as understanding, ratio-

---

178. Sidgwick, *Method of Ethics*, III. v.

nal beings.[179] But when we see him at work on his political system we find that he has obtained another premise, which is not
a consequence of those just mentioned. Men are "promiscuously born to all the same advantages of nature, and the use
of the same faculties."[180] Now in favour of this doctrine of the
equality of men's natural faculties Locke has scarcely a word to
say. This is the very corner-stone of Locke's politics; he quietly
assumes it. Whether Locke took it from Hobbes may be
doubted; but it is noticeable that this assumption is made by
our first psychologist, and had its origin in the psychologist's
belief that introspection gives us a clue to human action. At any
rate, it was not until the study of psychology was supplemented
by other studies that this belief was abandoned. The study of
history was not sufficient; Adam Smith had not freed himself
from it. That we now see it to be false is due chiefly to those
who have studied physiology as well as psychology.

Locke's denial of innate ideas and innate principles probably
led, though it did not drive him to this opinion. Though ante-
cedently to all experience a man's mind may be a blank, it does
not follow that the same external influences will produce the
same effects on all blank minds. It is not necessary to Locke's
argument against innate ideas that similar characters should be
formed by similar external circumstances acting on different
minds.

But after all, this matters little. Let us grant that all men are
equal at starting, must we say that they are always to be treated
as equals? Now, to say that those who come out of God's hand
as equals should always be treated as equals, is just specious; but

179. *Hum. Under.*, IV. iii. 18.
180. *Gov.*, II. iv.

there is a difficulty which stares Locke in the face. How are we to justify paternal power? Paternal power has been a standing protest against those who would found a system on natural equality. Locke has to admit that idiots, minors, and lunatics may be coerced without their consent being asked, and the reason he gives is, that such persons cannot know the law of nature. Those who have a natural right to be free and equal are those who have a capacity of knowing the law, and this capacity all men of the age of twenty-one and upwards have, and have apparently in an equal degree, if we except idiots and lunatics.[181] Now of this, his fundamental proposition, Locke gives no proof whatsoever, he gives no proof that our faculty of knowing the law of nature is not a matter of degree. If all men are, after the age of twenty-one, capable of knowing the law of nature, what are we to say of atheists, who, as Locke says cannot, or will not, acknowledge such a law? Filmer's editor is triumphant; *Solvitur Legendo!* is in effect his reply. All men equal? Who can write like Sir Robert? Locke's friends have a better right to such an argument. It is particularly strange that Locke should speak as if all men had an equal capacity of perceiving the law of reason, for he is rather fond of dwelling on the differences between the moral conceptions of different men, on the crimes which men can commit with "confidence and serenity," and has been reproved for so doing.[182] And even if we have equal faculties for perceiving the moral law (and it is on the universality of "reason" that Locke lays most stress) it does not follow that we have equal faculties for doing what we know to be right. Thus, even granting that all men are born with equal faculties, we must still

181. *Gov.*, II. 52, et seq.
182. *Hum. Und.*, I. iii. 9. Whewell, *Hist. Mor. Phil.*, Lect. v.

affirm that, at the age at which Locke would set them free from all government to which they have not consented, they are not equal in that faculty on which their conduct as citizens depends, much less in other faculties.

But it may be said that inequalities are adventitious, that when we came from God's hand we were all equal, and that this is evidence of God's intention. Without entering deeply into theology, we may surely urge, in the first place, that we have no reason to say that God willed the equality of babies more than the inequality of men. We must do one of two things, either we must ascribe all events to God's will, or only good events, and if we choose the latter alternative we must know independently what goodness is. On the first supposition we must say that tigers being God's workmanship ought not to be destroyed. On the second, if we accept Locke's account of good and evil, we must say that equality of political power is only willed by God when it is productive of pleasure.

But if there is little to be said for this argument as it is in Locke, there is less to be said for it as it is in Tom Paine. Locke says, "the taking away of God, though but in thought, destroys all." Truly it destroys his system; we can argue about the intentions of God, we cannot argue about the intentions of Nature, even when we spell Nature with a capital letter.

Mr. Spencer gets rid of one difficulty which troubled his predecessors, he denies a paternal right of coercion—we are to have a free nursery. In that complete democracy which he thinks the one passable form of government, lunatics, idiots, babies in arms are apparently to have the suffrage. Coleridge said that this was a legitimate deduction from the politics of pure reason. Perhaps he thought this a *reductio ad absurdum*.

Here appears one of the greatest difficulties which lie in the way of those who would transcend Utilitarianism, by setting up "the freedom of every man to do all that he wills, provided that he infringes not the equal freedom of any other man," as an Ideal of politics. For such philosophers hold that a purely democratic government "is the only one that is not intrinsically criminal,"[183] and yet they would find it hard to prove that such a government is the one most likely to acknowledge their supreme principle. If reason directs us both to pure democracy and to the greatest freedom of all, there is some chance of reason being self-contradictory. Here is an antinomy, the recognition of one portion of the rightful freedom of all may render improbable the realization of our complete ideal. What we should do in this case may be a question not of ethics, but of moral therapeutics, but it is one which fairly tests the practical value of a philosophy.

We have however arguments for equality of political power coming from a very different quarter, coming from the strictest sect of empirical Utilitarians.

To determine the best form of government was according to Bentham a very simple matter. What we want is that the rulers shall be those only whose interests are bound up with the interests of the people, this is "the junction-of-interests principle." Any rulers who are not answerable to the people will have sinister interests, which will take the place of general interests in their minds. He saw in pure democracy the one way of securing rulers who have no sinister interests. But the junction-of-interests principle would seem only fitted to secure "appropriate probity," and Bentham also required "appropriate intellectual aptitude," and "appropriate active talent." Blackstone himself

183. *Soc. Stat.*, ch. xx.

held that virtue is the characteristic of democracy, but that we require an admixture of monarchy and aristocracy to give us strength and wisdom. But Bentham thought that democracy will provide not only appropriate probity (virtue), but also appropriate intellectual aptitude (wisdom), and appropriate active talent (strength). In his *Catechism of Parliamentary Reform* he does indeed seem to doubt whether pure democracy will provide sufficient wisdom; he would allow the king to nominate certain members of the Assembly who should have a right of speech, though no right of voting.[184] But in his Constitutional Code, "Corrupter General" has vanished, and we hear little of intellectual aptitude and active talent. The one thing is to secure governors who have no sinister interests.[185]

The same theory, freed from all qualifications and thrown into a precise form, was elaborated by James Mill. The doctrine of his essay is so simple that it may be stated in a few lines. "The reason for which government exists is, that one man, if stronger than another, will take from him whatever the other possesses and he desires." There are three simple forms of government: monarchy, aristocracy, democracy. The two former are bad, because the rulers will engross all the materials of happiness. It might be thought that they would be easily satiable. But no, they are insatiable, for they require not only present pleasure but security for future pleasure. They will therefore attempt to reduce their subjects into a state of complete dependence. They will leave them but the bare means of subsistence, they will keep them in the most intense terror. Democracy has not the same evils, for the rulers being all, the interests of the

---

184. *Bentham's Works*, vol. III. pp. 542, 543.

185. Ibid., vol. IX. p. 3, et seq.

rulers are the interests of all. But democracy without a representative system is impossible. We should therefore try to obtain a representative government, which, by means of universal, equal suffrage, constant elections, and secret voting, should find its interest in acting in exactly the same way as that in which a complete assembly of the people would act, were it not too large to act at all.

This was an effort to construct a pure deductive science of government by the method of Hobbes. An attempt was made to justify it by citing the success of the same method when applied to political economy. Coleridge declared that a pure science of political economy was an impossibility; experience shews that he was wrong. But the pure deductive method which does seem applicable to the narrow subject-matter of plutology is inapplicable in the wider science of politics. We can make a supposition about the distribution of wealth never very incorrect, in the case of great commercial transactions absolutely true—Men will buy as cheaply and sell as dearly as possible. On the other hand, we have no one proposition about what all rulers will do, sufficiently true to be the basis of a pure science. Even if we admit that all men seek their own interests, this is only true because it is vague. It is obviously far less definite than the proposition from which pure plutology starts.

Least of all can we admit James Mill's axioms. He had taken his opinion of human nature from Mandeville and Hobbes, and thought it demonstrable that no king will be content until he has reduced his subjects into perfect slavery. It is certainly amazing that one who professed that he wished for the greatest happiness of the greatest number should have allowed no social impulses to any one else. If he imagined that were he king he could still be a well-wisher to mankind, the whole argument collapses. As it is, he falls into all sorts of absurdities. Only males of forty years old and upwards are to have votes. The interest of those under forty is taken to be identical with the interest of those over forty, and yet one man of forty will always, if not deterred by fear, take from another man of forty all that the latter has and the former desires. The fact is, that were men such as they are here painted, all discussion about government would be utterly in vain. Not only would the state of nature be a state of war, that is a trifle, it would be absolutely demonstrable that no other state could exist. What would be the first action of the representative assembly? It would be a step towards reducing the rest of the nation to slavery. Would they be kept in terror by the prospect of losing their seats? Would they not rather take care that there should be no future election? The people might thwart the attempt: but then, the people can thwart the attempts of a king or of an aristocracy.

Above all, who is it that will really make laws in a democracy? The majority. Then is it not absolutely certain that they will reduce the minority into slavery?

This objection is powerful, but it must be admitted that James Mill had some defence against it. Having assumed that, at any rate for the purposes of a science of government, we may look upon man simply as a being desiring the materials of happiness, he could maintain that in a democracy of such men there could never exist any permanent party divisions. There would be no permanent majority or minority. Combination to rob would have a limit. The poor majority would of course pass laws taking from the rich minority their wealth until wealth was equally distributed. Beyond this they would not go. When equality of power has given birth to equality of property, then all further combination would, on our hypothesis as to man's one motive, be impossible. *A* and *B* would have no more temptation for combining to rob *C*, than *A* and *C* have for combining to rob *B*, or *B* and *C* to rob *A*. An equal distribution of property would thus be a point of equilibrium.

But this shows the essential weakness of the position. The political combinations of which we read are seldom the results of a desire for wealth. Suppose that in the community the majority are Catholics, the minority Protestants, may not the former entirely exclude the latter from the possession of any legislative power? In such a case how would the Protestant be better off than if he were the subject of a Catholic prince? The laws made would be laws made by Catholics, not laws made partly by Protestants, partly by Catholics. The whole legislative force moves as the majority wishes, there is no diagonal between the ayes and the noes. Doubtless the grievances of the Protestants will be heard, and this is a real and powerful argument for representative government, men being what they are; it would be no argument at all were men such as James Mill described them. That the community "cannot have an interest opposite to its interests," is doubtless true, but that a majority of the citizens can have an interest opposite to the interests of the whole, is equally true, and far more important.

James Mill however would reduce his opponents to an absurdity, by saying that if men are not what he represents them, then there is no necessity for government. A more easily exposed fallacy was never given to the world. We want government not because all men are what he represents them, but because some men are something like what he represents all men to be. Were there but one thousand of his "men" in the country, we should require a government. But this would not do for James Mill, he must have a universal proposition or nothing.

What is true of one man is true of all; this assumption of the psychologists has been the bane of our political philosophy.

In his *Fragment on Mackintosh* Mill defended his *Essay on Government*. He actually cites Plato and Hume as witnesses for the defence, because they held that there should be some community of interests between the rulers and the ruled. There was no need to bring philosophic authority in favour of so common a common-place. The questions of his opponents, which James Mill had really to answer, were: (1) Is a community of interest between the ruler and the ruled all that you require—is it not necessary that the ruler should have the power as well as the will to rule well? (2) Is this power to be found in representative governments? (3) Can you prove that the interests of the majority and the interests of the whole must be identical? (4) Is it not demonstrable from your principles that peaceful government is an impossibility? (5) Has not your theory been contradicted by the whole course of history? In answering this last question "let him bethink himself of the age in which there was scarcely a throne in Europe which was not filled by a liberal and reforming king, a liberal and reforming emperor, or, strangest of all, a liberal and reforming pope."[186] There is scarcely a Tory who would not allow some force to the junction-of-interests principle, but there is not the slightest absurdity in believing with Plato and Hume, with men in general, that the ruler should be one who has the same interests as the ruled, and at the same time rejecting the democratic ideal.

As to the authority of Hume. Hume certainly says "political writers have established it as a maxim, that in contriving any system of government, and fixing the several checks and con-

186. J. S. Mill, *Represent. Gov.* (ed. 3), p. 15.

trols of the constitution, every man ought to be supposed a *knave,* and to have no other end in all his actions than private interest."[187] But common sense would tell us that we ought not to make our constitution one fitted only for perfectly wise and virtuous beings. The whole meaning of Hume's sentence depends on the meaning of self-interest. Interest is an elastic word. Hume would not have agreed to the following (which will shew how far James Mill could go). "We have seen that the principle of human nature, upon which the necessity of government is founded, the propensity of one man to possess himself of the objects of desire at the cost of another leads on by infallible sequence, where power over a community is attained, and nothing checks, not only to that degree of plunder which leaves the members (excepting always the recipients and instruments of the plunder) the bare means of subsistence, but to that degree of cruelty which is necessary to keep in existence the most intense terrors." It is further to be gathered from the context that the qualifying words "where nothing checks," mean "where no fear checks."

This argument for equality of political power, though in many ways so different from Locke's doctrine, has its origin in the same tendency, the tendency to overlook the differences between men. We see this tendency at work as soon as ever an attack is made on the doctrine of innate ideas. Hobbes expressly announces that introspection gives us the true clue to human action, history is worthless.[188] This was not necessary to Locke in his argument against innate ideas; but it was extremely natural to assume that all blank minds are the same.

187. *Essays,* I. vi.
188. *On Govt.,* III, pp. xi–xii.

Bentham and James Mill do not conclude from this that all men ought to be treated equally by introducing a theological doctrine; but the supposition colours all their philosophy. They could not conclude from this that all grown men when placed in the same circumstances will have the same desires, but they are led to exaggerate the force of external circumstances. Thus they do not contemplate the tyranny of a majority as possible, because they do not contemplate the possibility of there being in a democracy bodies of men with interests permanently conflicting. The external circumstances as regards matters of government are the same for all, therefore the desires of all as regards matters of government will be the same.

The love of simplicity has done vast harm to English political philosophy. The question of how far the interests of all men are harmonious is of fundamental importance, and yet our philosophers have failed to find a satisfactory answer, because they have assumed that the answer must be simple. English philosophy has here forgotten its usual caution; it has rushed from one extreme to the other. At one time it is ready to say that men are only kept from destroying each other by fear, at another that true self-love and social are the same. This comes of following the lead of Hobbes, of preferring to assume that all men are alike, to insisting that history must be called in to verify *à priori* theories. One of the strangest instances of this rushing into extremes occurred when Macaulay's Westminster Reviewer changed the principle of James Mill just discussed into an assertion, that the greatest happiness of the individual is in the long run to be obtained by pursuing the greatest happiness of the aggregate.

But the pupil may be excused when the master is inconsistent. Bentham, writing on international law, had said that there is a difficulty as to whose happiness the statesman should seek. Shall it be that of his subjects or that of the whole human race? The answer is, that practically the two are to be obtained by the same means. If a sovereign were to consult only his own subjects' happiness, he might think it necessary to serve other nations as he actually serves the beasts. "Yet in proceeding in this career, he cannot fail always to experience a certain resistance." He will find that the line of action which aims at the happiness of all nations is "the line of least resistance." "For, in conclusion, the line of common utility once drawn, this would be the direction towards which the conduct of all nations would tend, in which their common efforts would find least resistance, in which they would operate with the greatest force, and in which the equilibrium, once established, would be maintained with the least difficulty." These words are capable of overturning Bentham's theory of government. He admits that what is true of international relations is true of governmental relations. "The end of the conduct which a sovereign ought to observe relative to his own subjects . . . ought to be the greatest happiness of the society concerned. . . . It is the straight line—the shortest line—the most natural line by which it is possible for a sovereign to direct his course." Why so? Because "this is the end which individuals will unite in approving, if they approve of any."[189] What then becomes of our denunciation of kings and oligarchs? Why should their interests be always sinister when the line of least resistance, their most natural course, is that which leads to their subjects' happiness?

The fact is that neither opinion is true. Sometimes our line of least resistance leads to the public good, sometimes it does

189. *Principles of Internat. Law* (Works, vol. ii, p. 536 *et seq.*).

not. But Bentham had a hankering after mathematics, vagueness was an abomination, so he makes now one simple (and therefore improbable) supposition about human nature, and now another. On the whole, the longer he lived the less well he thought of mankind. The famous note, "So thought Anno 1780 and 1789, not so Anno 1814, J. Bentham,"[190] illustrates this change. It was a change for the worse, and James Mill was but too ready to go beyond Bentham, though even James Mill was very far from being consistent.

The essay by James Mill is important because it marks an epoch in the history of English philosophy. It was a grand attempt to found politics on empirical psychology unverified by history. At present it looks like a last attempt to fulfil what Hobbes proposed. Its extravagancies roused a storm of opposition. But it should be noticed that what was attacked was not Bentham's first principle that the greatest happiness of the greatest number is the one desirable end for all action, but his teaching about the dissonance of interests. The defeat of the Utilitarians (and they were defeated) was no triumph for the intuitive moralists. Let us take three champions of very different schools who attacked Mill's work. Macaulay was apparently a believer in Paley,[191] and shocked Mackintosh (who had recanted his Utilitarianism) by ethical heresies.[192] Coleridge was "a zealous advocate for . . . deeming that to be just which experience has proved to be expedient." Mr. Disraeli, in a defence of our constitution modelled on Burke, expressly says that it is not the Benthamite supreme rule which is objectionable, this is

190. Ibid., vol. i, p. 5.
191. *Essay on Westminster Reviewer's Defence.*
192. Mackintosh, *Hist. Eth. Phil.*, Note W.

really conservative, but the theory of the sinister interests of rulers. In fact the protest was directed against any attempt to found a pure science of government upon psychology. Coleridge pleads for the study of history, Macaulay for the Baconian method. We know now that it was this conflict of history and psychology which gave birth to the completest account of the logic of social science that we have. It was Macaulay's essay that roused John Mill from his trust in his father's geometrical method.[193] From the school of Coleridge he learned to value history. Then he arrived at his conception of the inverse deductive method[194] as the method of social science, a conception that has yet to be supplanted.

Some of James Mill's opponents erred in their enthusiasm for history. Macaulay would have found the pure Baconian method impracticable; he unfortunately set up Bacon's inquiry into the nature of heat as a model, an inquiry which Bacon's warmest friends condemn. Besides we have read that "That is the best government which desires to make the people happy, and knows how to make them happy. . . . Pure democracy, and pure democracy alone, satisfies the former condition of this great problem. That the governors may be solicitous only for the interests of the governed, it is necessary that the interests of the governors and of the governed should be the same. This cannot often be the case where power is entrusted to one or to a few." It was not James Mill who wrote this, it was Macaulay,[195] and yet the method of reasoning is scarcely Baconian.

The collapse of James Mill's theory marks one of the few

---

193. J. S. Mill, *Autob.*, p. 158.
194. *Logic*, VI. x.
195. *Essay on Mitford's History.*

great advances in English Political Philosophy. Since that time
we have heard little of one distribution of political power as
semper et ubique the only good one. Those who still argue that
there is but one form of government not criminal are not Utilitarians—not followers of Hume, but followers of Locke, Rousseau, and Coleridge's friend Major Cartwright. We have for the
most part returned to the position of Sir Thomas Smyth, "According to the nature of the people, so the commonwealth is to
it fit and proper,"[196] and we look for the nature of the people in
its history. We have got rid of the assumption of Hobbes that
for political purposes men may be treated as equals. It was necessary that the force of education should be brought into prominence, but our seventeenth century philosophers attended too
little to the original differences between men. Perhaps there is
some one form of government which will ultimately be found
the best for all communities, but any useful ideal of government
must be relative—relative to the people for whom we propose
it, relative to their history. John Mill's *Essay on Representative
Government* proposed a relative ideal, an ideal for the English
Constitution. James Mill's *Essay on Government* proposed an
absolute ideal. We may notice that by abandoning the traditional method, John Mill was brought to recognize many important facts hidden from our earlier philosophers; such, for
instance, as the immense influence which government exercises
on the life of the nation outside the sphere of direct governmental interference. This led to a new plea for a wide distribution of power as a means of education.

Of Coleridge's peculiar doctrine of representation we must
speak very shortly. He professed to discover from history that

196. *De Republicâ Anglorum*, p. 17.

"the idea" of English government consisted in a representation of the interests of permanence and progression. The landed interest—"the realty"—is the interest of permanence; the personal interest—"the personalty"—is the interest of progression. This "idea," whatever else it is intended to be (and this is not clear, for Coleridge, in his Kantian moments, declares that an idea expressed in words is always a "contradiction in terms") is also an ideal. We are to strive to realize the idea in any alteration of our constitution. Looking then at Coleridge's idea of a state simply as a constitution to be aimed at, we find it open to the gravest objections. The exact proposal was that the House of Lords should be taken to represent the realty, that the suffrage should be so distributed that the majority of seats in the Lower House should belong to the personalty, the realty having a strong minority.[197]

(1) A representation of interests as opposed to a representation of numbers (against which Coleridge rages)[198] comes to mean a representation of classes, for the law can only take notice of obvious external distinctions. Surely it is bad to insist on the discord of class interests unless it is absolutely necessary; legal recognition of the discord will aggravate it.

(2) The distinction of interests into permanent and progressive is bad. There never has been a party which could make standing still its whole programme. We all want to move, but we want to move in many different directions. The real conflict is not between those who would stand still and those who would move, but between those who would go this way and those who would go that.

197. *Church and State.*
198. *Table Talk,* 19 Sept., 1830.

(3) Had Coleridge known more of that political economy which he despised and called semi-infidel, he would have seen that to place in one class landlords, tenant-farmers, and agricultural labourers, in another lawyers, capitalists, artizans, and others, is a thoroughly worthless distinction. Whether a man gets his income from land or not is quite unimportant; the really important question is, What influences does his income depend on? Coleridge would have found that the agricultural labourer and the artizan have much more interest in common than the agricultural labourer and the farmer. The old distinction of high and low, rich and poor, goes nearer to the root of the matter than that of realty and personalty.

(4) Some of the personalty have no peculiar interest in progression. The conveyancer's interest is more allied to permanence of a particular kind than even the landowners.

(5) Some of the realty have no peculiar interest in permanence. Coleridge puts together the contentment of the wealthy landowner and the obdurateness of prejudice against change "characteristic of the humbler tillers of the soil." But while wealthy men will probably be tolerably contented whether they be landowners or not, he would be a rash man who trusted to the agricultural labourers, now that communication is easy, showing any peculiar aversion to change. The fact is, Coleridge was led away by the talk of the Protectionists, who made believe that farmers and agricultural labourers would be injured by free trade. How wrong they were is well evidenced by the fact that the once familiar phrase "the landed interest" has dropped out of our political vocabulary.

(6) Coleridge should have known that human interests are not so simple as James Mill thought them; he was here following the school which he disliked. Men do not want to vote only

in their economic character, they want to vote as Churchmen, as Dissenters, as Total Abstainers, as friends of Peace at any price. The line dividing the realty from the personalty does not even roughly coincide with some of the most important distinctions. The consequence would be that in Coleridge's scheme some men, *e.g.* merchants, would be refused votes because if they had them their class would be over represented. A merchant will say that he does not want to vote *quâ* merchant but *quâ* Ritualist, and he will feel his exclusion as arbitrary. *Some* merchants must be left out; but why should it not be his Evangelical neighbours? Unless some such arbitrary lines are drawn, the results of Coleridge's plan would coincide with those of a representation of numbers.

A consideration of the complexity of interests at greater length would bring us to the conclusion that, in a community fully conscious of the way in which it is governed, no system of representation can be stable which does not proceed on few and simple rules. Every addition to the number of rules leads to distinctions which must be felt as arbitrary. All changes in our representative system which are to be final or successful will be movements towards greater simplicity, not necessarily towards greater simplicity in the machinery of election, but towards greater simplicity in the distribution of voting power. We shall move towards the scheme advocated by John Mill, not towards the scheme advocated by Coleridge. It might be different could we label men as belonging to different "interests," but this becomes more and more difficult every day.

Harrington started an interesting line of speculation when he said that the balance of power depends on the balance of property, and it is a pity that this has not been followed up. His own theory was far too simple, he thought monarchy in England had become impossible because landed property was so widely distributed; it proved otherwise. Still we may say that any change in the balance of power which is not brought about by force, and which is not a restoration, will tend to place the balance of power in the same hands as the balance of property. We can say also that equality of political power tends to produce equality of property, for where there are no hereditary distinctions one motive for saving is absent. But unfortunately we have no speculations on this subject.

In the early days of our political philosophy, the right to property was not made the matter of such frequent dispute as the right to rule. There was less difference between practical men as to the former right. But even in the days of Hobbes there were levellers abroad, who "were casting how to share the land among the godly, meaning themselves, and such others as they pleased."[199] They looked for the speedy establishment of the fifth monarchy; there was among them that religious enthusiasm which might have made socialism possible. Even Harrington, who was no enthusiast, would set a limit to property in the interests of popular government. Hobbes of course could defend existing property law, as he could defend all existing law; we have consented to it. The great continental jurists also made consent, or occupation and consent, the foundation of a right to property. Locke however tried to find a title to property independent of consent, for he wished to insist that this was one of our rights which had not been surrendered to the legislative body. He deduces it from the common right of all men to the gifts of God, and the exclusive right of every man to his own labour.

199. Hobbes, *On Govt.*, VI. 365.

The gifts of God to be used must be consumed, and con-
sumption involves appropriation.[200] Things must be considered
appropriated when labour has been spent upon them. He shows
clearly that much of the value of wealth is due to labour, and
holds that the propriety of labour overbalances the community
of land. Hallam contrasts this "excellent chapter" most favor-
ably with the teaching of Grotius and Puffendorf, and the "pu-
erile rant of Rousseau."[201] "That property owes its origin to oc-
cupancy accompanied with labour is," he thinks, "now generally
admitted." What property owes its origin to is one question,
what is its justification is another. These questions Locke, in
the manner of his age, confounds; but he certainly meant to
give not only an historical account, but a deduction of right.
He thinks that in former times, when there was enough for all,
"right and conveniency went together"; before the invention of
money (the influence of which Locke always exaggerated) men
had no temptation to enlarge their possessions beyond their
wants. But (and here he abandons his first theory) since the
invention of money, "it is plain that men have agreed to a disproportionate and unequal possession of the earth; they having,
by a tacit and voluntary consent, found out a way how a man
may fairly possess more land than he himself can use the product of." So after all, Locke rests the natural right to property
as it at present exists on a tacit consent, evidenced by the use
of money.

Dr. Rutherforth, who belonged to the English Grotian
school, criticized Locke's theory with justice.[202] He thinks that

200. *Civ. Gov.*, II. 25–51.
201. *Hist. Lit.*, IV. iv.
202. *Institutes*, I. iii. 10.

even if Locke can show that labour has a title to 99/100 of the value of property, there is still a 1/100 part to which labour has no right; it comes from nature. He lays stress on Locke's falling back upon consent, and argues that consent, evidenced by occupation, is the real foundation of the right. Thus both Locke and the Grotians, in the last resort, rely on a title by tacit consent.

Such was the state of the argument when Rousseau began his tirade against inequality. He would not recommend a return to natural equality; he only wishes for a state in which no man is so rich as to be able to buy another's labour, no man so poor as to be bought.[203] Still, if "buying" mean "hiring," this is a long step towards levelling. He allows that labour may give a title to property, but it must be labour, not a mere marking out of the ground. This argument has been repeated by Paley.[204] Though Rousseau's historical account is far inferior to Locke's, he could have driven the latter into very awkward positions. Locke's argument seems only just as long as there is "common" to be reclaimed. What! are we "promiscuously born to all the same advantages of nature," only to find all nature's gifts engrossed? Why is a tacit consent enough in this case, when the social compact requires "express promise and contract"? "Men have agreed to a disproportionate and unequal possession of the earth." What men? Do the promises of parents bind their children? Locke says they do not. Let us make the consent a reality. Enough of fictions. Let the landowners shew that they have laboured, or that we have consented.

Meanwhile Hume produces another justification of property, its utility. But Hume allows that "wherever we depart from . . .

203. *Soc. Cont.*, II. xi.
204. *Mor. Phil.*, III. iv.

equality we rob the poor of more satisfaction than we add to the rich."[205] The rule of equality is useful, and has been shewn by history to be not wholly impracticable; but perfect equality we cannot have. "Render possessions ever so equal, men's different degrees of art, care, and industry will immediately break that equality. Or if you check these virtues, you reduce society to the most extreme indigence." This is the line of defence behind which Paley and Bentham took their stand.

Then Hume asks that question which his opponents find it so hard to answer. What is property? Now if Locke is not to fall into pure Hobbism, he must find some criterion by which we may judge any scheme of property law. What ought to be a man's property? Shall we allow devise, bequest, inheritance? If so, let us put to Locke the question which Locke put to Filmer. Who is heir?[206] We know who is heir according to English law, but who is heir according to the law of nature deduced from the ideas of God, and of ourselves? Here let us quote Locke himself. "There being no law of nature, nor positive law of God, that determines which is the right heir."[207] . . . No law of nature on so important a point! Then is the law of nature our sole criterion of right and wrong? How are we to justify English property law, since the law of nature will not answer the very simplest question as to the extent of the natural rights of property? There is an escape; we may say with Locke that "the public good" (*i.e.* pleasure) "is the rule and measure of all law making"; then we are at one with Hume.

Paley followed Hume closely in his justification of property, but he brought into relief the weak side of the Utilitarian argu-

---

205. *Inquiry . . . Morals*, III. i.
206. *Civ. Gov.*, I. 106.
207. Ibid., II. i.

ment. The institution of property is, he thinks, "paradoxical and unnatural." The fable of the pigeons seems to lead to levelling principles. Inequality is admitted to be an evil, but it is a necessary evil; it flows from rules by which men are incited to industry. "If there be any great inequality unconnected with this origin it ought to be corrected."[208]

Bentham agrees. There is a *prima facie* argument in favour of equality. On this subject he tries to be very precise. His theory as set forth in the *Principles of the Civil Code*,[209] and more accurately in the *Pannomial Fragments*,[210] is that if we go on adding to a man's wealth, to the sum of material objects of desire of which he has the use, each increment of wealth produces an increment of pleasure, but the pleasure never increases so rapidly as the wealth. It follows that the distribution of a given amount of wealth, which produces most pleasure, is an equal distribution. This may be looked upon as a cardinal doctrine of Utilitarianism, for Hume, Paley, Bentham, and Mill are agreed upon it. But none of these teachers recommend any very serious measures for obtaining this equality. Before we can estimate their reasons for narrowing the sphere of this doctrine we may see what attempts have been made to obtain an equation connecting wealth-produced happiness with wealth. Now we have two probably independent attempts to perform this feat. Bentham says, "It will even be matter of doubt whether ten thousand times the wealth will in general bring with it twice the happiness."[211] Paley says that it ought to be assumed that ten persons possessing the means of healthy subsistence possess a

208. Ibid., III. 2.
209. *Works*, I. 304.
210. Ibid., III. 228.
211. Ibid., III. 229.

greater amount of happiness than five people however wealthy.[212] This agreement is striking. The wealth-produced happiness of the richest is never twice the wealth-produced happiness of a man who has the means of a healthy subsistence. How large an admission of levelling principles this is can easily be shown in a rough way. Let us take £100 per annum as a means of a healthy subsistence. There are in this country 8500 incomes of £5000 and upwards; these, if cut up into incomes of £100, would produce more than twenty-five times as much happiness as they now do.

What has Paley got to say against this strong case? According to him the principal advantages of such a property system as ours are that: (1) It increases the produce of the earth; (2) It preserves the produce of the earth to maturity; (3) It prevents contests; (4) It improves the conveniency of living, by permitting a division of labour and by appropriating to the artist the benefit of his discovery. These may all be summed up in what Hume says in the passage quoted from him. To which Hume adds that equality of possessions weakens authority by leading to equality of power. Bentham's defence is by far the most powerful, he insists vigorously on the supreme importance of security. The evils which would follow from constant redistributions (alarm, danger, the extinction of industry) would throw the good of an equal distribution into the shade. "Equality ought not to be favoured except in cases where it will not injure security; where it does not disturb expectations to which the laws have given birth; where it does not derange the actually existing distribution." Bentham's *Essay on the Levelling System*

212. Ibid., VI. xi.

contains all these arguments repeated in their most telling form.

But what is remarkable is that we have not yet come across the Malthusian argument. I would not say that Bentham and Paley fail to resist the enormous prejudication which they have raised in favour of equality, but on their own principles it would have been difficult to reject a proposal made by Tom Paine.

Paine was the most popular of English demagogues, and justly so, for he came out of his controversy with Burke (who was hampered by the conventional theory) without serious loss. This being so, it surprises us to find that Paine was but little of a socialist. Indeed, socialism was not a product of 1789, but rather of 1830 and 1848. Paine was a leveller, not a socialist, and a comparatively moderate leveller. He would but establish a national fund out of which £15 should be paid to everyone on arriving at the age of twenty-one, and £10 per annum to every person over fifty years of age "to enable them to live without wretchedness, and go decently out of the world." He considers agrarian laws unjust, for the greater part of the value of land is due to labour; still there is some portion of the value due to nature, and on this the tax should be thrown.[213] Locke's premises lead to this, if we exclude title by consent.

What we may ask would Paine's scheme necessitate? Supposing our present population to remain constant, a tax of about 6 per cent. on all incomes over £100 would suffice. Now supposing this scheme was introduced with great caution, supposing that it was only to come into force after the lapse of a generation, I think Bentham and Paley would be put to it to find objections, if they chose to abide by their principle.

213. *Agrarian Justice.*

Of course such a tax would diminish wealth. But all that Bentham and Paley can say is that a man will not work for others as he works for himself. The rest of Paley's objections need not apply; there need be no insecurity, no uncertainty, no contests. How much the motives to industry would be diminished by such a tax we can scarcely guess, but it would need a perfectly preposterous assumption to show that wealth would be so much diminished, that the great advantages of an equal distribution would be overbalanced. It is all very well to say that the rich would *consume* their wealth instead of *saving* it, and thus there would be no wages, demand for commodities not being demand for labour; but we must not let the phrases of economists drive us into absurdities. What way is there in which the rich can use by far the greater part of their wealth without paying wages, or inducing someone else to pay wages? One and one only, they can waste their wealth without obtaining any enjoyment from it.

Against socialism, with its attendant uncertainty, Paley and Bentham have a very good defence, a defence which will be sufficient until some considerable change in human nature has taken place. But to considerable steps towards levelling, to taxing the rich for the relief of the poor, they cannot fairly object. As to Paley, one chapter in his work is the best apology for levelling ever made.[214] He holds that the improvement (*i.e.* increase) of population is "the object which ought, in all countries, to be aimed at in preference to every other political purpose whatsoever." He devotes a chapter to suggesting means to this end, he actually goes out of his way to revive the moribund fallacy of the balance of trade, because he thinks that the "ac-

214. *Works*, VI. xi.

cession of money" increases population, he would add to our species by adding to our specie. Paley's principles justified Pitt in saying, "Let us make relief in cases where there are a number of children a matter of right and honour, not of opprobrium."[215] Pitt framed a bill providing that people should be paid for bringing children into the world. The bill was withdrawn, thanks, it is said, to the criticism of it which Bentham sent to Pitt.[216] Bentham's editor, Dumont, gives to Bentham the credit of anticipating Malthus,[217] but he is scarcely warranted in so doing; indeed, though Bentham did not think with Paley that legislative interferences are required in order to make the population increase sufficiently quickly, he never (as far as I know) used the Malthusian argument.

If we compare this chapter of Paley's with the ordinary talk of our own time, we find how completely new the most popular modern justification of property is. The subject of population is one on which Plato and Aristotle had speculated, but it was strangely neglected in England. Malthus really drew attention to a class of facts which had been ignored by all preceding English theorists. Nor did he assume his principles as convenient hypotheses; he had a stronger sense of the value of history than has been granted to most of our philosophers. He sought to prove from history that the "positive checks" on population have been in constant operation. We have here only to inquire how much he added to the Utilitarian defence of a property law such as ours. It must be allowed that if the increase of population was due to causes over which we have no control, Paley

---

215. Quoted by Ricardo (*Pol. Ec.*, ch. v).
216. *Works*, I, Preface, 70. VIII. 440.
217. Ibid., III. 73.

and Bentham would lead us to some vigorous scheme of levelling. In Paley's case this is obvious. If to increase the population be the first and foremost duty of a statesman, Malthus
might well ask Paley how he could spend his time in devising
petty changes in our laws when Paine had recommended so
much more efficient a route to the desired end. "Accept Paine's
advice," he might say, "and you will have your heart's desire: the
country will swarm with men and women."

Modern socialism has always seen in Malthus its most for-
midable enemy, and Malthus' first opponents found no way to
answer him save by an audacious denial of the fact that population was increasing.[218] The fact is that there was a strong superstition which Malthus had to resist. Providence, it was thought,
will take care that population does not increase too fast. Godwin held that "there is a principle in human society by which
population is perpetually kept down to the level of the means
of subsistence."[219] Yes, said Malthus, there is such a principle,
the principle of starvation.

Malthus showed that to insure to every person the means of
subsistence would cause a rapid increase of population. But this
was not enough. It might be argued that every man would still
have as good a chance of extracting a livelihood from nature
as had his fathers. But here comes in Malthus' principle that
population tends to increase faster than the means of subsistence, which means this, that as long as our means of coercing
nature remain what they are, we can only extort an addition to
our supply of food by a more than proportionate addition to our
labour. Now here we have a really new argument against lev-

218. *E.g.,* Cobbett, *Pol. Regist.,* 10 April, 1823.
219. *Pol. Justice,* VIII. iii.

elling, an argument which Malthus and Ricardo made too much of when they pleaded for the abolition of the poor laws, but an important addition to the armoury of Bentham and Paley. I do not however believe that even with this addition Bentham and Paley would be safe. It might be said that even allowing for an immense increase of population, a great decrease in the incitements to industry, and full force to the law of diminishing returns, the supposition that the richest man has never twice as much wealth-produced happiness as the poorest man, leaves an ample margin for levelling principles. It might further be urged that there are pleasures to which the law of diminishing returns does not apply, such are the pleasures of family society. Again, Godwin founds his plea for equality, that plea which occasioned the reply of "the Arch-Priest of Famine" (as Godwin's son-in-law called Malthus), not so much on the desirability of lessening the pains of physical want as on the desirability of getting rid of "the spirit of oppression, the spirit of servility, and the spirit of fraud," which are "the immediate growth of the present administration of property." On the other hand, Malthus, by showing how fast population might increase if a bounty was given, did show that redistribution must be frequent, and thus added new force to Bentham's argument against insecurity.

It is doubtful whether Paley and Bentham could logically defend such a property law as ours without modifying what they say about the connection between wealth and happiness. I may not enter into verbal criticism, but neither philosopher sufficiently recognized the possibility of a man's wealth-produced happiness being a minus quantity. When Bentham says that ten thousand times the wealth does not bring twice the happiness, he seems to assume that the wealth-produced happiness of a man who has no wealth is zero; but this is untrue, it is a very large negative quantity. Let us first attend merely to the happiness which results from the use of "material objects having a value in exchange," or "wealth-happiness." If we decrease a man's wealth below a certain point, his wealth-happiness becomes a minus quantity, he suffers the pain of want. Further, let us remark that Paley much underrates the connection between wealth and happiness in general; a certain minimum of wealth is necessary as a condition for any happiness. The pain of starvation excludes all or nearly all pleasures. From the consideration of the possibility of a man's wealth-happiness being a minus quantity, we may come to think that though ten men with £1000 a year are together far happier than one man with £10,000, yet one man with £100 per annum is happier than ten men who have but £10 a piece to last them through the year. But does not this add new force to the argument for equality? Yes, if we consider only persons in *esse*. No, if we consider persons in *posse*. No, if our scheme will ultimately increase the number of those whose wealth-happiness is negative. Suppose a Utilitarian had an annuity of £1000 and there were nine existing persons who had nothing, we should go even further than Paley in recommending an equal distribution; it will save much suffering. But suppose a Utilitarian has an annuity of £1000 and no children, we should say that he ought perhaps to wish for nine children who might share his wealth, but not for 99, certainly not for 999. If however we do not admit the possibility of wealth-happiness being negative, if we hold by the letter of what Bentham and Paley have said, we must admit that 1000 persons with £1 per annum a-piece are together more than fifty times as happy as ten persons with £100 per annum a-piece.

And this, when we consider that some wealth is a necessary condition for almost every class of pleasures, seems absurd.

The Utilitarian can perhaps scarcely get to any precise theories on this subject, he can only point to the quarters from which the good and evil effects of measures promoting equality will come. The fact that there is doubt on such subjects as the connection between wealth and happiness, is a terribly strong argument against Bentham's scheme of a political arithmetic. But still we know that there is a general argument against inequality, an argument valid in the absence of other Utilitarian arguments, an argument admitted every time that our Court of Chancery says that equality is equity. This argument would be one of great force in any discussion of our present law of inheritance. On the other hand, we know whence the evils of a levelling scheme will flow.

Unsatisfactory principles no doubt to the believer in neat theories, but where, let us ask shall we look for better? Locke will not help us, for, though he can deduce a right to property from the law of nature, he cannot tell us whether that right includes the right of inheritance. Hutcheson will not help us, for he becomes Utilitarian. Our English moralists will not help us, for since the writers on the law of nature gave way before the Scotch psychologists, scarcely one anti-Utilitarian moralist has treated of politics. Even Dr. Whewell will not help us, for he gives no criterion by which we may judge different schemes of property law, and Dr. Whewell is one of the few English moralists who have attended to the morality of law.

One refuge remains. There is Kant, who to some extent formulated the doctrines of "natural jurisprudence." Here we have his account of what ought to be property. "Das aüssere Meine ist dasjenige ausser mir, an dessen mir beliebigem Gebrauch mich zu hindern, Läsion (Abbruch an meiner Freiheit die mit der Freiheit von Jedermann nach einem allgemeinem Gesetze zusammen bestehen kann) sein würde."[220] Now how could we use this in constructing a law of property? Kant admits testamentary power; but what testamentary power? It is surely evident that if the law of equal freedom allows of bequest at all, it allows of settlements in perpetuity.

Let us once more refer to Coleridge. "Now," he says, speaking of this very doctrine, "it is impossible to deduce the right of property from pure reason."[221] Then follows this note—"I mean, practically and with the inequalities inseparable from the actual existence of property, abstractedly, the right of property is deducible from the free agency of man. If to act freely be a right, a sphere of agency is so too." I suppose this "practically" and "abstractedly" means that we can from the fact of free will deduce that there ought to be *some* proprietary rights, but that we must appeal to expediency to know *what* rights, for (as Coleridge has just told us) whatever is expedient he deems to be just.

Coleridge was a Utilitarian in politics because he was a Conservative. He escaped out of Kant's system just in time, for what would a supporter of "the realty" have said to Mr. Spencer's use of the Kantian principle as destructive of a right to property in land?

220. [My external property is that outside of myself regarding which any hindrance in my discretionary use would be a violation (diminution of my freedom, which can exist with the freedom of everyman together with a general law).] *Rechtslehre.*

221. *The Friend,* Essay IV.

A distinction between property in land and property in other things has been common. It has been supposed that a justification good for the latter is not good for the former. This is due partly to the distinction between *mobilia* and *immobilia* which every code naturally makes, partly to the distinction between realty and personalty, the result of the conflict in this country between feudalism and commercialism, above all to the superstition that nature helps agriculture more than any other industry. This superstition is ancient, in modern times it formed the foundation of the physiocratic economy, it hampered Adam Smith, it crops up where one least expects it.

The physiocrats used this doctrine to account for the fact of rent. Thus Paine could say that rent is not due to labour or capital, but to nature; therefore the levelling tax should be a rent-charge. This was correct on Locke's principles, for had not Locke admitted that a part of the produce of land is due to nature, and must not this part be the rent? When Bastiat came to deal with Paine's successors, with all his cleverness he made one unfortunate admission. If Ricardo's theory be true, then property in land is unjust. Ricardo's theory most certainly is true, all Bastiat's ingenuity notwithstanding. Here is the difficulty of admitting that labour alone gives a title to property. Bastiat can only escape by playing upon the word "service."

Next we will take Mr. Spencer's deductions from the law of equal liberty.[222] He says: "Given a race of beings having like claims to pursue the objects of their desires, given a world adapted to the gratification of those desires, a world into which such beings are similarly born, and it unavoidably follows that they have equal rights to the use of this world. . . . It is manifest

222. *Soc. Stat.*, X and XI.

that no one or part of them may use the earth in such a way as to prevent others from similarly using it; seeing that to do this is to assume greater freedom than the rest, and consequently to break the law." This certainly seems a correct deduction from the law of equal freedom, and Kant must give up the right to landed property. But cannot we go further? Let us change the argument. Given a race of beings having like claims to pursue the objects of their desires, given an apple adapted to the gratification of these desires, an apple near which such beings are similarly born, and it unavoidably follows that they have equal rights to that apple. . . . It is manifest that no one or part of them may eat that apple in such a way as to prevent others from similarly eating it; seeing that to do this is to assume greater freedom than the rest, and consequently to break the law.

Mr. Spencer would have the society constitute itself the supreme landlord. He argues that the law of equal freedom is not broken in this case, for every man has an equal power of becoming tenant. Certainly every man would have an equal power of becoming tenant if every man could offer an equal rent, but what of this? Every man has now an equal power of becoming a landlord, if every man can offer an equal price.

Then there comes this *reductio ad absurdum* of "landlordism." If one man may be the rightful owner of any part of the earth's surface, some few men might have a right to exclude all their fellows from the world. But it is not obvious that we can also say that if one man has an exclusive right to any one particle of matter, some few men may have a right to all matter.

But these arguments can scarcely be serious. If the law of equal freedom condemns land-ownerism it condemns coat-ownerism also. Touch not, taste not, handle not, make haste to leave this world lest you infringe the equal rights of others; this is the law of equal freedom.

But then there is an apparently solid argument. "We daily deny landlordism by our legislation." The railway and canal acts are appealed to as evidence of this. Now Mr. Spencer holds a leasehold tenure to be just, a freehold tenure to be unjust. He appeals to popular opinion as supporting him. Here we can apply a really crucial test. If popular opinion as evidenced by Acts of Parliament makes any difference between wrongful and rightful tenures, these Acts will treat the leaseholder in a different way from that in which they treat the freeholder. Do they do so? Certainly not: a company has just the same power of compelling a tenant for years at a competition rent to sell his interest, that it has of forcing a tenant in fee to sell his estate. If we deny "landlordism" we deny land-tenantism also. The reason why land is more often made the subject of compulsory sale than are other things is obvious, and has nothing to do with the law of equal freedom. In case of war our government might very likely force shipowners to sell their steamships; it would deny shipownerism, if ships were wanted for public purposes, just as it denies landlordism and land-tenantism when land is wanted for a railway.

But Coleridge also drew a distinction between property in land and property in other things. "It is declared by the spiritual history of our laws that the possession of a property not connected with especial duties, a property not fiduciary and official, but arbitrary and unconditional, was in the sight of our forefathers the brand of a Jew and an alien; not the distinction, nor the right, nor the honour, of an English baron or gentleman."[223] This is the Idea of our law of real property. Towards the Idea, "the line of evolution, however sinuous, has still tended . . . sometimes with, sometimes without, not seldom

223. *Church and State*, p. 49.

against, the intention of the individual actors, but always as if a power greater and better than the men themselves had intended it for them."[224] The Idea is not only the point towards which evolution has tended, but it is also an ideal, an object to be aimed at by us. Now whether property in land ought or ought not to be absolute and unconditional may be an open question; but if the spiritual history of our laws declares that a fiduciary and official property in land is the point to which evolution has tended, the spiritual history of our laws must have some little difficulty in accounting for facts. Indeed, it must state what is, temporally speaking, exactly the reverse of the truth. There has been through long centuries a tendency at work making the law of realty more and more like the law of personalty. True, we still say that no subject can be the supreme lord of land, but what is now the merest fiction was once a great reality, and that reality disappeared bit by bit. Little by little the power of alienation and the power of testamentary disposition were won. When the legislature would not move fast enough popular opinion permitted the judges to evade the very words of statutes by all manner of fictions, fines, recoveries, and so forth. Surely these powers of disposition are the signs of absolute as opposed to fiduciary possession. Take again the extremely gradual extinction of manorial rights. These were "connected with especial duties," but they have disappeared. Coleridge sometimes asserts that the idea of property in land is a new one. This also is untrue. It is an idea which has very slowly evolved itself through the course of our history. Nor could Coleridge say that it appeared during the reign of the false philosophy. No, it came in during the ages which he loved.

224. Ibid., p. 35.

The great statute which converted all tenures into free and common soccage was older than the days of Locke. From the Statute of Fines to the last Land Transfer Act there has been one steady tendency in all legislation on the subject, a tendency to assimilate the law of real property to the law of personal property. It may be that this tendency has been from good to bad. It is open for Coleridge to say that this has been the case; but it should be admitted by all that if property in land is to be made less a matter of commerce than property in other things the tendency of centuries must be reversed.

Mill prophesies that it will certainly not be much longer tolerated that agriculture should be carried on (as Coleridge phrases it) on the same principles as trade.[225] This may be so, but this prophecy must be founded on other grounds than a history of our law, however "spiritual."

To consider the now common arguments for making a distinction between property in land and property in other things would be to transgress our limits by entering on post-Coleridgean controversy. But it may be remarked, that if we rigorously exclude the old physiocratic fallacy, and perceive that the law of equal freedom cannot make any distinction until it is supplemented by some doctrine as to the way in which restraint must be measured, the controversy is not one which can be decided by a bare appeal to first principles, but requires much economic and historical discussion.

225. *Essay on Coleridge.*

The Body Politic

I hope that you will forgive me for choosing a subject which lies very near to that which Sidgwick discussed at our last meeting. I had thought of it before I heard his paper, and though to my great delight he said some things which I had long wanted to hear said, his object was not quite that which I have in view. He spoke of the means, the very inadequate means, that we have of foretelling the future of bodies politic. I wish to speak of the means, the very inadequate means as some people seem to think them, that we have of filling up the gaps that at present exist in our knowledge of the past history of these political organisms. The two processes, that of predicting the future and that of reconstructing the past are essentially similar, both are processes of inference and generalization. Of course when the historian tells us a single fact, for example, gives the date of a battle, inference and generalization are already at work. He has got this supposed fact from (let us say) some chronicler or some tombstone, and he has come to the conclusion that about such a matter this chronicler's or this tombstone's word may be trusted. But when he goes on to represent as usual or rare some habit or custom or mode of thought or of conduct he is very obviously drawing general conclusions from particular instances, and is, if I may so say, predicting the past.

Sidgwick drew a distinction between empirical and scientific predictions. I will apply this distinction to postdictions. I did not gather from him that he meant to draw a hard and accurate line between the empirical and the scientific. Certainly for my purpose I could not draw it with a firm hand. But still though we have before us a matter of degree the distinction is real and important. The historian of the old-fashioned type who does not talk about scientific method or laws of nature is drawing inferences and making generalizations, but these do not as a general rule go far outside the country and the time that he is studying. We may compare him to the chancellor of the exchequer who is estimating the produce of next year's taxes. Sometimes the two procedures are very strictly comparable, as when the historian who thinks that he has examined enough accounts ventures on a general statement about the revenue of Henry II or George III. Now in a certain sense it is true that the method employed in these cases ought to be a scientific method, that is to say, it ought to be the method best adapted to the purpose in hand. Still it is only scientific in the sense in which the method of a Sherlock Holmes would be scientific. The end of it all is a story, a causally connected story tested and proved at every point. Also it must I think be allowed that history of this old-fashioned kind is successfully standing one of those tests of a science that Sidgwick mentioned last time. No historian dreams of beginning the work all over again. Even if he has a taste for paradox and a quarrelsome temper he accepts what is after all the great bulk of his predecessor's results. Men are disputing now whether the forged decretals were concocted in the east or in the west of France, whether they shall be dated a little after or a little before 850; the man who attributed them to the popes whose names they bear would be in much the same position as that which is assigned to the man who says that the world is flat; he would be taking up arms against an organized body of knowledge. I should doubt whether books about the most rapidly advancing of the physical sciences become antiquated more rapidly than those books about history which do not belong to the very first class.

Now to this progress I do not think that we can set any narrow limits. During the present century there has been a rapid acceleration. Tracts which were dark are now fairly well lit and neglected and remote pieces of the story are being systematically explored. Of course I am including under the name of history what some people call archaeology; for to my mind an archaeology that is not history is somewhat less than nothing, and a Special Board for History and Archaeology is like a Special Board for Mathematics and the Rule of Three. Whether we fix our eyes on the east or the west, on ancient or modern times, we see that new truths are being brought in and secured, and this in that gradual fashion in which a healthy body of knowledge grows, the new truth generally turning out to be but a quarter-truth and yet one which must modify the whole tale.

But this process, rapid as it seems to me (for I am comparing it with the growth of historical knowledge in the last century), seems far too slow to some who compare it with the exploits of the natural sciences. They want to have a science of history comparable to some of those sciences, and, for choice, to biology. A desire of this kind there has been for a long time past; in our own day it has become very prominent and there are many writers and readers who seem to think that we are within a measurable distance of a sociology or an inductive political science which shall take no shame when set beside the older sciences. Having a science of the body natural we are at last to have a similar science of the body politic. The comparison of a state or nation to a living body is of course ancient enough. The Herbert Spencer of the twelfth century worked it out with grotesque medieval detail; the John of Salisbury of our own century teaches us that the comparison is just about to become strictly scientific since we have at last an evolutionary biology. Now the suggestions derived from this comparison have been of inestimable value to mankind at large and to historians in particular. I wish once for all to make a very large admission about this matter. But for this comparison, the vocabulary of the historian and of the political theorist would be exceedingly meagre, and I need not say that a rich, flexible, delicate vocabulary is necessary if there is to be accurate thinking and precise description. For the presentation—nay, for the perception—of unfamiliar truth we have need of all the metaphors that we can command, and any source of new and apt metaphors is a source of new knowledge. The language of any and every science must be in the eyes of the etymologist a mass of metaphors and of very mixed metaphors. I am also very far from denying that every advance of biological science, but more especially any popularization of its results, will supply the historian and the political theorist with new thoughts, and with new phrases which will make old thoughts truer. I can conceive that a century hence political events will be currently described in a language which I could not understand so full will it be of terms borrowed from biology, or, for this also is possible, from some science of which no one has yet laid the first stone. But I think that at present the man studying history will do well not to hand himself over body and soul to the professor of any one science; that if in one sentence he has spoken of political germs or embryos or organisms, he will not be ashamed to speak in the next of political machinery and checks and balances. He may write of the decay, death, dissolution of the Roman empire, but at times he will not contemn the classical decline and fall.

But I ought to be speaking not of metaphor but of method. Now were there to be any talk of scientific biology I would at once end this paper with a confession of blank ignorance, but my contention is that we ought not to believe ourselves to be within sight of such talk. To me it seems that if we start with the comparison suggested by such phrases as "body politic" or "social organism" we are not within sight of that sort of knowledge that every old woman in a village has and has long had of the human body. She knows truths about the span of life, about the growth of children, about their teething, about gray hairs, old age, and death, the like of which we do not know, and so far as I can see are not going to know about the parallel social phenomena, if any such parallel phenomena there be. In effect she judges from time to time that some child is not in a normal condition, though she does not use the word "normal." She sends for the doctor, or, may be, living in Devonshire, she sends for the seventh son of a seventh son. No matter what she does, no matter how absurd may be the remedies that she tries, she knows that normally a baby's body is not covered with scarlet blotches. Have we brought, are we likely to bring our inductive political science up to this high level?

Take the best known truth about the life of man, the old major premiss, "All men are mortal." Take a generalization which aims at greater precision, "The days of our years are three score years and ten." Now among our sociologists I seem to see a great unwillingness to grapple with this somewhat elementary question. Are all states or nations mortal? Have you any phenomenon which is parallel to natural, as contrasted with violent death? Sidgwick touched this point last time, mentioning the case of the Roman empire. Now I should agree with him that if in this context we are to speak of death at all, it must be of violent death; "she died in silence biting hard among the dying hounds." But biting and struggling in the strangest fashion so that when the turmoil is over we hardly know which is dead, the Roman wolf or the German wolf-hound. If really we are to apply this metaphor of death to the events of the fifth century we shall I think have to eke out the vocabulary of biology with that of psychical research. After a while we see, to use Hobbes' splendid phrase, "the ghost of old Rome sitting crowned upon the ruins thereof." But when did the ghost become a ghost? Of course we must not ask the sociologist for anything so unscientific as a precise date. I don't want to pin him to 476 or to 1453 or to 1806, besides the question seems to me a foolish one. That a historian may now and again find it well to speak of the Empire perishing or dying in the fifth century I would not deny— though the contemporary history of what has once been even if it is not still the Eastern half of a single body politic will warn him that this analogy has difficulties before it—but I am sure that he will not ride his metaphor very far without a fall, and I don't think that biology is going to dictate a peace to the scholars who are quarrelling bitterly as to the revival of Roman organization in Merovingian Gaul.

I suppose that sometimes a political organism of a low kind, some tribe or horde does cease to exist in a fashion that we can with no great strain of language compare to a natural death; but I cannot think of any instance in which this figure of speech could be consistently elaborated for the purpose of describing the disappearance of a political organism of a high type, and I see no reason whatever for the belief that the bodies politic which we know as France, Germany, and so forth must grow feeble and die if they are not destroyed from without.

There are many other questions that I should like to ask. How are we to picture some such historical events as the partition of Poland, the transfer backwards and forwards between France and Germany of lands which in a neutral language are called Alsatia and Lotharingia, the peopling of North America by men of many different races. Poland we say is torn to pieces and devoured. Yes but for a long time the undigested fragments of it which lie in three separate stomachs are striving to be one again. The Irish in North America have a for us most unfortunate habit of regarding themselves as part of the Irish nation. This cross-organization, if I may so call it, is one of the great difficulties. The man who is an Englishman if you please but first a Catholic bids us pause, for surely we are sticking in the very bark of our social science and becoming the slaves of that militancy that Mr. Spencer detests if we will have no organisms except such as are defined for us by international lawyers. Of course the history the Catholic church gives us is by far the grandest instance of a super-national or extra-national organization. But we have not seen the last of phenomena which in one respect we may call similar. We have not I fear seen the last of a super-national or infra-national organization of anarchists, whose doings are likely to produce remarkable changes in the police organization of various countries. We see too the beginnings of many societies which aim, it may be at the spread of science and learning, it may be at the encouragement of sport, but which neglect national boundaries. If we have a long peace before us all this may become of great importance. We may be destined to hear "An Englishman if you please but first a professor of sociology in the University of Man."

Now that complication and interdependence of all human affairs of which we find a by no means solitary example in this cross-organization gives as one of the reasons why we are not bringing our generalizations about social organisms up to that standard of precision that the old woman has attained when she speaks to us of life and death and the teeth of babies. It seems to me that those who are talking most hopefully about sociology are constantly forgetting the greatest lesson that Auguste Comte taught, though I cannot say that his practice came up to his preaching. I mean the interdependence of human affairs, for example the interdependence of political, religious, and economic phenomena. It seems to me that the people who have learnt that lesson are not the sociologists but the historians. If I may make a guess, and it is here that they would find their defence against a criticism which, if I remember rightly, Sidgwick passed upon them, namely that in their keen hunt for new discoveries they neglect what after all are the important matters. They would I think say—We do not yet know except in the roughest way what are the important, the causally important matters, only this we know for certain that they were neglected by even the greatest of our predecessors. Even if you only wish to study political organization (giving to political its narrowest sense), you are perforce compelled to study a great many other phenomena in order that you may put the political into their right places in a meshwork of cause and effect. You may for instance write a political or constitutional history which says very little of religion, or of rents and prices. Life is short; history is the longest of all the arts; a minute division of labour is necessary. No one man will ever write of even a short period of that full history which should be written if we are to see in all completeness the play of those many forces which shape the life of man, even of man regarded as a political animal. And therefore I think it is that some of the best because the truest history books are those which are professedly fragmentary, those which by their every page impress upon the reader that he has only got before him a small part of the whole tale. That is the reason why, though history may be an art, it is falling out of the list of fine arts and will not be restored thereto for a long time to come. It must aim at producing not aesthetic satisfaction but intellectual hunger.

All this by the way. The fault, so it seems to me, of the would-be scientific procedure of our sociologists lies in the too frequent attempt to obtain a set of "laws" by the study of only one class of phenomena, the attempt for example encouraged by this University to fashion an inductive political science. Too often it seems to be thought that you can detach one kind of social phenomena from all other kinds and obtain by induction a law for the phenomena of that class. For example it seems to be assumed that *the* history of *the* family can be written and that it will come out in some such form as this: We start with promiscuity, the next stage is "mother right," the next "father right," and so forth. Or again take the history of property— land is owned first by the tribe or horde, then by the house-community, then by the village-community, then by the individual.

Now I will not utterly deny the possibility of some such science of the very early stages in human progress. I know too little about the materials to do that. But even in this region I think it plain that our scientific people have been far too hasty with their laws. When this evidence about barbarians gets into the hands of men who have been trained in a severe school of history and who have been taught by experience to look upon all the social phenomena as interdependent it begins to prove far less than it used to prove. Each case begins to look very unique and a law which deduces that "mother right" cannot come after "father right," or that "father right" cannot come after "mother right," or which would establish any other similar sequence of "states" begins to look exceedingly improbable. Our cases, all told, are not many and very rarely indeed have we any direct evidence of the passage of a barbarous nation from one state to another. My own belief is that by and by anthropology will have the choice between being history and being nothing.

If we climb a little higher the outlook for science is far more hopeless. If the creator of the universe had chosen to make a world full of compartments divided by walls touching the heavens, had put into each of those cells a savage race—if at some future time the progress of science had enabled men to scale these walls—I won't say but that this would have been an interesting world. We imagine the inquirer passing from cell to cell, examining the present state of its inmates, exploring their past history as recorded by documents which range from the chipped flint to the printed book. After a while he begins to know what he will find in the next box—"Ah! I thought so, promiscuity, group-marriage, exogamy—fetishism, polytheism, monotheism, positivism—picture writing, ideogram, phonogram, ink, block-books, movable type—the old tale." After a while he has got a law—What, no evidence of a polytheistic stage in this country. I supply that stage with certainty; the evidence must have been lost. He comes to a more puzzling case where twist the evidence how he will it breaks his law. But by this time he is justified in using such terms as "morbid," "abnormal," "retrogression"—here is a diseased community and he will investigate the climate of the cell and so forth in order to get at the cause of the disease. There remain many compartments with walls so high that they are still insurmountable. "Considering my many thousands of observations," he says, "I feel entitled to make a scientific prediction as to what is behind these barriers—in some cases I shall be wrong and to details I will not commit myself—but in general I shall be right."

A very interesting world this would be, but exceedingly unlike the world in which we live. In the real world the political organisms have been and are so few and the history of each of them has been so unique that we have no materials apt for an induction of this sort, we have no means of forming the idea of the *normal* life of a body politic. Not to speak of the biologist's materials we are not within sight of materials of that kind where our villagers have drawn their rude laws of life. We do not know, if I may so put it, that Siamese twins are abnormal. A funny comparative anatomy we should have had if the only living things that the men of science had seen were those collected in the booth of a fair—the two-headed nightingale, the pig-faced lady, and the five-legged donkey. Of course I am exaggerating if I take the monstrous assembly as a fair representative of the family of nations. Nations have much in common, but then a very great part, an indeterminately great part of what they have in common is the outcome of deliberate imitation. Of course I am aware that human beings imitate each other and that within limits they can modify the structure of their bodies by this imitative conduct—but I do not think that those who know about this matter will contradict me if I say that these modifications are trivial when compared with the changes produced in bodies politic by the analogous process. Mr. Leslie Stephen has compared the acquisition by a state of a new kind of artillery to the acquisition by an animal of new and stronger teeth. The modern state says, "Go to! I will have strong teeth because another state has got them"—and straightway within a year the teeth are there. A superficial change, we may say, is to be compared with the acquisition of artificial teeth. Yes, but what a series of social changes a new weapon may set up. I read, and I suppose this to be a plausible theory, that one of the most decisive steps in that process which we call the feudalization of Gaul, and therefore of western Europe, was the outcome of an effort to obtain a cavalry able to cope with the Saracen horsemen and is it not trite that the invention of gunpowder has profoundly modified our social and political organization.

I will take an example of imitation. Near the end of the last century England had a criminal procedure that was all her own, trial by jury. I believe that I am right in saying that there was then nothing that resembled it in any country, at all events in any country that was at all likely to be taken as a model by other states. The difference was great; the whole civilized world was against us. Our procedure was public, accusatory, contradictory, theirs was secret, inquisitory, and relied on torture—the same procedure in all its main features was common to all states in the western half of Europe. And then country after country copied, deliberately and professedly copied us. Now I am very ready to allow that if England had never existed the continental procedure which was stupid and cruel would sooner or later have been destroyed, but I do not see the remotest probability that a jury or anything resembling a jury would have been introduced. I am not praising the constitution of ours; I am not at all certain that foreigners might not have done better if they had not copied it; but copy it they did and at first in minute detail. I am also very ready to admit that deliberately copied institutions rarely produce in their new home all the good that is expected of them and often turn out to be failures. I am quite willing to believe, for example, that this pretty new constitution of Japan will break down—I do not mind saying, though I know little that entitles me to say, that the Japanese have tried to skip too many stages—but of one thing I feel moderately certain, namely that they can never return to the place where they were in 1850, and that the great attempt to be European will for a very long time to come give shape and colour to the whole history of Japan. To what changes in the body natural can we liken these changes.

And this sort of thing has been going on since the remotest past. How pleasant it would be to have a natural history of one of the chief of those instruments which have modelled the body politic. I mean the alphabet. How nice to say you start with pictures, you pass to ideograms, to phonograms, to letters. Have we four instances of the completed process, have we three, have we two? I do not know, but the number of alphabets which were regarded as independent has been decreasing very fast of late—and now I suppose it to be established that the Egyptian alphabet is the mother of a very numerous family. Would the Greeks have evolved an alphabet if they had not borrowed from borrowers—and what changes must we not introduce in Greek political thought and political practice—and therefore in the political thought and practice of the whole western world in later times—if we deprive Greek thinkers of the alphabet.

For this reason if we are to talk of organisms at all it seems to me expedient that we should very often regard the whole progressive body of mankind as a single organism—I feel inclined to add: and as one infected by that strange, that unique disease called civilization which is running through all its organs, always breaking out in fresh places, and the end whereof no man has seen. And for this reason it is that I have a special dread of those theorists who are trying to fill up the dark ages of medieval history with laws collected from the barbarian tribes that have been observed in modern days. This procedure urges me to ask, If these tribes of which you speak are on the normal high-road of progress why have they not by this time gone further along it? If I see a set of trucks standing on a railway line from week to week, I do not say, This is the main up line to London, I say, This must be a siding. The traveller who has studied the uncorrupted savage can often tell the historian of medieval Europe what to look for, never what to find, for the German or the Slav hardly appears upon the scene before he is tainted by the subtlest of all poisons.

For one last illustration may I return to criminal procedure. Perhaps I exaggerate its importance but on the whole I think that if some fairy gave me the power of seeing a scene of one and the same kind in every age of the history of every race, the kind of scene that I would choose would be a trial for murder, because I think that it would give me so many hints as to a multitude of matters of the first importance. Well, are we to have some law as to the normal development of judicial organization in its higher stage, if so which piece of history are you going to treat as typical for that stage of progress which our modern nations covered between let me say 1100 and 1789? Is it to be the English or French, they are radically different. If we regard the mere number of persons or the mere number of nations that stand on the two sides, there can be no doubt that we must decide in favour of the French. I believe that a certain amount of generalization is possible here—that the current of changes in Italy, Spain, Germany, and the Low Countries flows in the same direction as the current of changes in France, though France leads the way, and there is a great deal of deliberate imitation of French institutions. A very careful French historian with this problem before him has pointed to a course of divergence and I have little doubt that he has pointed in the right direction. Of all these countries at the critical time, say between 1150 and 1300, Britain was the only one in which there was no persecution of heretics, in which there were no heretics to persecute. Everywhere else the inquisitory process fashioned by Innocent III for the trial of heretics becomes a model for the temporal courts. I do not think that this is the full answer. If I were to say more I should have to speak of the causes which made the England of the twelfth century the most governable and the most governed of all European countries, for if a Tocqueville had visited us in 1200 he would have gone home to talk to his fellow-countrymen of English civilization and English bureaucracy. However there can I think be no doubt that we have laid our finger on one extremely important cause of divergence when we have mentioned the Catharan heresy. Behind that stand Bulgarian monks and so we go back to Manes. Or if we ask why this faith becomes endemic in the south of France we have to explore the political and economic causes which had made Languedoc a fertile seed-bed for any germs of heresy which might be blown thither from any quarter. Now the question that I have proposed seems to me one which cannot be answered and should not be asked. The history of judicial procedure in England seems to me to be exactly as normal as the history of judicial procedure in France or in Germany, or (to put it another way) the idea of normalness is in this context an inappropriate and a delusive idea; it implies a comparison that we cannot make. What I have said about judicial procedure might I think be said also, with the proper variations, about governmental and legislative organization. The history of the parliament of Westminster is neither more nor less normal than the history of the parliament of Paris. But a science of bodies politic which knows nothing of the normal or the abnormal—which cannot apply either of these adjectives to the process which made a Louis XIV the absolute king that he was, or the process which subjected William III to the control of a house of commons—seems to me a science falsely so called and one which must expect to hear from the other sciences—"Well you don't know much and that's a fact."

That is the reason why when I see a good set of examination questions headed by the words "Political Science" I regret not the questions but the title. Each question if anything more than the loosest, vaguest, baldest answer is expected is really a question about some specific piece of history, and I regret the suggestion that names and dates may properly be omitted. For example a question about the causes of feudalism seems to me to be a question about a certain specific piece of Frankish history, though no doubt a full answer would say something about the causes which prepared other nations to receive willingly or unwillingly certain Frankish institutions. The answer would not be the worse for saying a word about Japan—but so far as I can learn from some commended book on Japanese history I think it should say that of the origin of the so-called feudalism of Japan next to nothing is known and that men who profess to know what is known say nothing about that precarious tenure of land by warriors which I had thought to be the very essence of Frankish and therefore of European feudalism in its first stage. I do not regret the questions—on the contrary it seems to me very desirable that under whatever name youths should be taught as much history as possible—but I do regret the suggestion that at the present time the student of history should hope for and aim at ever wider and wider generalizations.

INDEX

This book is set in 11 on 14 Caslon. William Caslon designed
the face in the early eighteenth century, modelling it after
Dutch types of the late seventeenth century.

Printed on paper that is acid-free and meets the requirements
of the American National Standard for Permanence of Paper
for Printed Library Materials, z39.48-1992. ∞

Book design by Erin Kirk New,
Athens, Georgia
Typography by Graphic Composition, Inc.,
Athens, Georgia
Printed and bound by Sheridan Books, Inc.,
Ann Arbor, Michigan